WOMEN ENTREPRENEURS ONLY

12 WOMEN ENTREPRENEURS TELL THE STORIES OF THEIR SUCCESS

GREGORY K. ERICKSEN, ERNST & YOUNG LLP

John Wiley & Sons, Inc.

New York · Chichester · Weinheim · Brisbane · Singapore · Toronto

This publication is designed to provide accurate and authoritative information in regard to the subject matter covered. It is sold with the understanding that the publisher is not engaged in rendering legal, accounting, or other professional services. If legal advice or other expert assistance is required, the services of a competent professional person should be sought.

Library of Congress Cataloging-in-Publication Data:

Ericksen, Gregory K.
    Women entrepreneurs only : 12 women entrepreneurs tell the stories of their success / by Gregory K. Ericksen : Ernst & Young, LLP.
        p.   cm.
    "Profiles from the Ernst & Young Entrepreneur Survey conducted in September 1998"—P.
    Includes bibliographical references.
    ISBN 0-471-32439-6 (cloth : alk. paper)
        1. Self-employed women—United States—Case studies.
    2. Entrepreneurship—United States—Case studies.
    3. Businesswomen—United States—Case studies.   4. Success in business—United States—Case studies.   I. Ernst & Young.
    II. Title.   III. Title: Women entrepreneurs tell the stories of their success.
    HDB072.6.U5E74   1999   98-55274
    338'.04'082—dc21   CIP

Ch. 1: Photography by Dennis Full.
Ch. 2: Photography by Oxmoor House, 1998.
Ch. 3: Photography by Paul Rico.
Ch. 4: Photography by Jeff Barlowe.
Ch. 5: Photography by Douglas Elbinger.
Ch. 7: Photography by Glenwood Jackson.
Ch. 8: Photography by David Lorne Photographic.
Ch. 9: Photography by Diversified Photo, Plainview, NY.
Ch. 10: Photography by Giddings.
Ch. 12: Photography by Dementi-Foster Studios.

Printed in the United States of America.
10 9 8 7 6 5 4 3 2 1

CONTENTS

21.21

ACKNOWLEDGMENTS

This book represents a collaboration by many talented people to whom we owe our thanks. First, we are especially grateful to the 12 women entrepreneurs who are profiled here. They stand out as much-needed role models for what it takes to go forward, venture—and succeed. They took time out from their demanding schedules to share their experiences, know-how, and insights. Each not only tells an individual story that illuminates the emergence of women in business, but also epitomizes what it means to be an entrepreneur, with all the incredible variety that this entails. There are others to thank. The board members of the Entrepreneur of the Year® Institute provided support and guidance. Phil Laskawy, chairman of Ernst & Young LLP, as well as my colleagues at E&Y, particularly the National Marketing Department, have encouraged this project from its very beginning. As always, my wife, Gina, and family, continue to support my work. At every stage of this book, Andrea Mackiewicz has provided an editorial eye and direction. Edward Wakin, with his invaluable research and writing efforts, has brought this project to fruition. Thank you all.

Gregory K. Ericksen
Dallas, Texas

INTRODUCTION

In the emerging era of entrepreneurship, the 1990s have become the decade of women entrepreneurs. They no longer command attention because they are unusual, but because they are important. They are no longer seen as followers but as leaders, no longer viewed as confined to certain businesses, but as innovators across the full range of business and commerce. Their emergence is a worldwide phenomenon, as noted at the fifth Global Summit of Women by Sakiko Fukuda-Parr of the U.N. Development Program: "The growing economic power and influence of women-owned businesses are changing the shape of the global economy."[1]

Nowhere is the phenomenon more pronounced and more dramatic than in the United States where close to 8 million women-owned businesses employ one in four U.S. company workers and contribute nearly $2.3 trillion

[1] Fifth Global Summit of Women was held in London, United Kingdom, in July 1998. The statement made by Sakiko Fukuda-Parr was quoted in "Women's economic power growing quickly," an article by Edith M. Lederer.

annually to the economy. Over the past decade their employee rolls have tripled and their sales have more than tripled. There's more to come. Women-owned businesses are increasing at nearly twice the national average and those with more than 100 employees are growing at a rate six times the national average.

Beyond recognizing the phenomenon, there's much to learn about entrepreneuring by looking closely at individual women, each unique and distinctive in her own right and also representative of all entrepreneurs. Each provides a case study and a model of how to succeed as an entrepreneur. This is particularly revealing when women entrepreneurs agree to *tell the story of their success* by talking freely and openly about their work, their experiences, and their lives—as in this collection of 12 profiles. The results are enlightening answers to questions about women entrepreneurs that apply to all entrepreneurs:

> What are they like?
> How did they get started?
> What were their biggest challenges and how did they
>   overcome them?
> How did they create their successes?
> What motivates them?
> Who helped them most and how?
> What would they have done differently if they knew
>   then what they know now?
> What do their lives as entrepreneurs mean to them?
> What can we learn from their success stories?
> What advice do they have for aspiring entrepreneurs?

Out have come revelations in their own words that go beneath the surface, bring their successes to life, and place their accomplishments in perspective.

The carefully selected cross section of women presented in this book reflects the variety and range of women with *a business of their own.* They demonstrate that the world of business is, by no means, a man's world, but a world in which customers rule and products and services reign over the fortunes of companies. The entrepreneurs represented in this cross section have not only succeeded in areas traditionally considered as a woman's domain (nursing, home products, home and office cleaning), but also in areas traditionally considered male territory (real estate, restaurants, moving, minor-league baseball). The immediate lesson is that it's not who you are, but how you meet customer needs and wants that makes the difference.

Nothing dramatizes the emergence of women entrepreneurs like the process of selecting 12 women to profile from the outstanding entrepreneurs Ernst & Young has honored over the past 12 years in 47 regions and in 12 national categories. There have been women in electronics, venture capital, ergonomic seating, helicopter transportation for offshore oil drilling, technology for the disabled, construction, computer education, auto parts, credit cards, residential management, and ambulance service, only to cite a random sample. The list goes on and on, as varied as the U.S. economy.

Essentially, all entrepreneurs are the same. Basically, they create business where there was no business before, whether they transform a company or start one. They combine energy, initiative, determination, timing, and talent. They know what to do with "luck" when it comes their way, which is another way of identifying their ability to recognize opportunity and take advantage of it. The Roman philosopher, Seneca, stated it succinctly: "Luck is what happens when preparation meets opportunity."

As the profiles in this book demonstrate, there are no gender boundaries in the basic makeup of entrepreneurs. The women profiled in this book epitomize the list of the "Top 10" characteristics of all entrepreneurs as identified by U.S. influentials in a survey commissioned by Ernst & Young:[2]

1. Recognizes/takes advantage of opportunities
2. Resourceful
3. Creative
4. Independent thinker
5. Hard worker
6. Optimistic
7. Innovator
8. Risk taker
9. Visionary
10. Leader

Women add to these characteristics the experience of being daughters, wives, and mothers. As such, they have been pioneers in combining work and family, an issue that has become prominent in recent years for everyone in the world of business. They lead the way in showing how to achieve balance in personal lives while reaching the heights of business success. They bring to the work/family issue their own versions of commitment, concern, and personal responsibility.

They have also demonstrated that opportunity is found wherever the enterprising personality engages the world around. In the case of Sheryl Leach, it was as a young mother who came up with the blockbuster idea for the legendary children's favorite, Barney. Joy Mangano as a housewife developed the Miracle Mop. A single mother like Mary Ellen Sheets started by helping her sons earn spending money and ended with a nationwide company for local moving franchises. Dorothy White turned to cleaning houses to supplement her family income and

[2] The Ernst & Young Entrepreneur Survey was conducted in September 1998 by Roper Starch Worldwide of influential Americans (defined as people who in the past year participated in three or more items from a list of political and social activities).

ended up with a multimillion-dollar commercial cleaning service. All of them are reminders that entrepreneurs start anywhere and their ideas pop up everywhere—in a traffic jam, on a park bench, in the kitchen.

When a survey was conducted of women and men business owners, the findings reflected what is evident in these profiles.[3] Women start new businesses because they are inspired by an entrepreneurial idea. The next most frequent reason is frustration with their previous work environments. Most women either start a business totally unrelated to their previous jobs or turn a personal interest into a business pursuit. As to their greatest rewards, they cite being their own boss and having greater freedom.

The women portrayed in this book reflect what is evident among successful entrepreneurs. They find fulfillment in what they do. They enjoy their work. It's what they would rather be doing. At 88 years of age, Ebby Halliday still is at it, running a $2.5 billion residential real estate firm: "I've always looked upon work as a privilege and that's why I'm still at it. They say that nothing is work unless you'd rather be doing something else. There is nothing else I want to do."

As company leaders, these women entrepreneurs epitomize human relations. They share their enthusiasm, demonstrate their commitment, and are unstinting with their energy. The characteristic culture they cultivate is directed toward teamwork and sharing. They combine personal touches on a day-to-day basis with a policy of giving opportunities to the people who work for them. The examples range from cooking breakfast for their headquarters staff or ordering in pizza for everyone to their promotion policies and employee stock plans. On one

---

[3] "Paths to Entrepreneurship: New Directions for Women in Business," survey released on February 24, 1998, by Catalyst, the National Foundation for Women Business Owners, and The Committee of 200.

hand, they are entrepreneurs who happen to be women. On the other hand, as women they recognize the importance of personal relations with the people who contribute to their success. They mean business, but also gravitate toward a family style in which their people work with them rather than for them and are recognized as having a first name and a personal, as well as work, life.

Women demonstrate that success does not depend on a large investment, particularly if you are a woman facing a reluctant banker. As one study has found, women entrepreneurs have succeeded with a median investment of $10,000 to $25,000, only one-quarter of it borrowed. For the entrepreneurial-minded, women provide memorable Horatio Alger examples, as illustrated by these 12 women and captured by signature remarks that sum up their philosophy of doing business:

- *If you do a good job, someone will notice.*
- *We've made service our priority.*
- *The kind of care giver I would want for my mother.*
- *The best coffee in the world and service with a smile.*
- *We're creating memories for people.*
- *I'm always thinking about different ideas to try.*
- *The product is always king.*

More than ever, entrepreneurs demand attention. The Ernst & Young survey found that nearly 8 out of 10 influentials have designated entrepreneurialism as "the defining trend of the business world in the next century" and project that most Americans will engage in entrepreneurial activity at some point in their lives. Just as the nineteenth century was viewed as the Industrial Age and the twentieth century as the Corporate Age, the twenty-first century looms as the Entrepreneurial Age, with women entrepreneurs, such as the ones profiled here, as major players.

1

SHERYL LEACH—BARNEY

"Business Is Common Sense"

SHERYL LEACH—BARNEY

"Business Is Common Sense"

Sheryl Leach, a stay-at-home mother in Plano, Texas, was caught in a traffic jam in 1987 and thinking about what it took to entertain her one-and-a-half-year-old son who had—appropriately—the attention span of a one-and-a-half-year-old. He hardly gave her a breather, a chance to make a phone call, or even to make a cup of coffee, until she learned about a video called *We Sing Together.* The video, which ran for a full hour, mesmerized him and got her thinking.

Sitting there behind the wheel of her car, surrounded by impatient motorists on a Texas freeway, she was struck by an entrepreneurial "Eureka." "I had an idea to do a video." At the time, the idea hardly qualified as a blockbuster, but it certainly does 10 years later. It was the birth of Barney, the world's most popular children's entertainer, the smiling purple dinosaur who comes to life to play and sing with preschool children. In the 10 years since the first Barney video in 1988, more than 45 million Barney home videos have been sold in the United States alone, in addition to millions abroad. Since the television debut of *Barney & Friends* in April 1992, it has become

3

the No. 1 TV show in America for children under six, and it is seen by children in more than 80 countries on six continents.

That's not all. Barney Music is the third-largest children's music label in the industry. Twenty-seven Barney books have made the *Publishers Weekly* best-seller list among 103 Barney titles, which have sold 80 million copies. Barney has also been a hit on the theater circuit: his musical stage show has been a sellout in 60 cities. For good measure, Barney products—toys, games, apparel, bedding, accessories, and snack foods—are selling around the world, but particularly in the United States where more than 90 percent of children under six have Barney products at home.

. . . It always takes a dedicated team behind anything to make it happen. Nothing great is ever accomplished by one person.

Then there's the full-length theatrical motion picture, *Barney's Great Adventure: The Movie.* Its director, Steve Gomer, has a daughter and son who, appropriately, became Barney fans and so is he: "Barney is such a good soul. He is always positive, always cheerful. Who could ask for a better [movie] star? He's the sort of friend we would all love to have, supportive and nurturing. All the things you need to be surrounded by if you are a kid or even as an adult, for that matter."

Yale University's Family Television Research & Consultation Center agrees. After a series of studies on *Barney & Friends,* the Center's researchers found that the show has a very positive educational impact on young children.

They concluded that it's "nearly a model of what a preschool program should be."

The Barney phenomenon makes the traffic jam moment worth recalling, not only as a dramatic reminder of how entrepreneurial ideas break out anywhere, but how a successful entrepreneur pulls together personal skills, circumstances, and experiences and takes advantage of opportunities. When all the parts and pieces are put together in retrospect, there can be an inevitability about what entrepreneurs come up with and succeed in doing, even though Sheryl Leach maintains, "I would say that I never really thought of myself as an entrepreneur." But if she weren't an entrepreneur at heart, her interior monologue would have been just a daydream in a traffic jam one sunny afternoon in Plano, Texas.

> *I was in my car, alone, stuck on the freeway, thinking about how my son was so very active. I had made a decision to stop working and to be at home with him for his first two years. He was just so active that I had very little time to call my own. He was very, very demanding. Then I discovered through other moms that there was a video out on the market called* We Sing Together *that was very sought after. It was not in the big video rental places and it was not in the big mass merchandising stores. It was sold in small, independently owned educational stores. This video was educational, with lots of singing and dancing. So I got one and it changed my life. Suddenly, my son—instead of only doing something for five minutes and then crying—sat for a whole hour and was entertained by the singing and dancing. He loved the video and I felt good about it because it was also educational.*
>
> *Having been a teacher—studying childhood development and educational theory—I thought it was impossible for a child one-and-a-half to two years old*

to sit for an hour. That was supposed to have been impossible. So I thought about what was happening and said to myself that something here is breaking all the rules that I had accepted as truth. While stuck there in traffic, I thought about what happened with the video. My son played it and played it and played it. He'd seen it so many times that he was beginning to outgrow it. I had thought: "No problem. I'll just go get another one." When I went back to the store, the owner said the company that did the video was coming out with a second one, but there was a long waiting list for it. Otherwise, she said, there was really nothing else out there that works with very small children.

I thought about what she said while sitting in the traffic jam and my marketing brain started to kick in. I thought well, there's a long waiting list. . . . here's a product that works like nothing else. . . . there are millions of parents out there like me and millions of two-year-olds out there like my son. It's such a difficult age. If there could be a product designed specifically for that age group that would hold their attention, something parents felt was good for them as educational, and specifically designed to hold their attention, it would be a win-win.

At this point, Sheryl followed what she now identifies as three basic "factors," which she recommends for entrepreneurs:

1. There has to be a demand.
2. There has to be an excellent product to satisfy the demand.
3. There has to be a strong belief in the product.

"To me, business is common sense," she says. "And good business is even more strongly common sense, because there's a logic, a rhyme and reason the way business operates and the way human beings operate."

What I have found—which could help other entrepreneurs—is that when you have an idea and believe in it, it's almost like the whole world conspires to help you.

Already certain of the demand for the right video, Sheryl set out to develop the product that "two-year-olds would love and parents would thank God for." Her starting point was a successful product—*We Sing Together.* She analyzed what happened when preschoolers watched the video, and she made a mental checklist of what worked and what didn't, noting when preschoolers clapped and sang and when they were bored or walked away from the television. She checked what was on the screen against children's reactions: "My ideal was to take all the things that worked and put them into a video series that was bound *to be a better mousetrap.*"

I felt as an educator and as a parent that the video did some things that worked very well, but some things I felt could be improved. Today, we call them our success elements. There are about 17 elements that we have identified since I brought on other people to build a team which has been very instrumental in helping me develop the list and make Barney a success. As far as I am concerned, it always takes a dedicated team behind anything to make it happen. Nothing great is ever accomplished by one person. From the start, one of the most obvious things is that very young children love to watch things that are familiar to them in their world. That's common sense, simple and very self-evident. They love music. They love colorful things. They love to watch other children. And very young children prefer live action to animation.

Sheryl's traffic jam daydream didn't stop at identifying the product. She started to think about the *producer.* Who could do it? Who could turn out a product that would satisfy the demand that's out there? Who had the range of skills and experiences that must come into play?

As I thought about how successful such a video would be, I began thinking about what kind of person could produce such a video. I thought that it would be great if the person were a parent, because the parent of a child that age knows what works and what doesn't. Then I thought it would be really helpful if the person could have been a teacher, because teachers know something about developmental psychology. It would be great if the person were a writer and also had a background in marketing, as well as sales and distribution.

Then came the dawning. Sheryl was describing *herself,* starting with her experiences as a 35-year-old mother of a son in the restless age. In college, she had studied education at Southern Methodist University and after graduation taught art and music in San Antonio, where she also was a volunteer teacher of English as a second language for recent immigrants. Her next stop was Dallas, where she was an instructional leader at an inner-city elementary school and earned a master's degree in bilingual education from East Texas State University. Her next stop was the American School in Guadalajara, Mexico, where she went to teach and to become fluent in

Spanish. She returned to Dallas and became a freelance writer handling a range of writing projects, including assignments for a publishing company called DLM (Developmental Learning Material). She met her husband at DLM, which is his family-owned and -operated business. After their marriage, they moved to Chicago, where he worked in the company's printing operation, and Sheryl became director of public relations for a Chicago inner-city hospital.

When DLM offered her a position as director of sales, marketing, and distribution for educational software the company wanted to develop, Sheryl branched out in a new direction. (It also turned out to be her preparation for launching Barney in the home video market.) She became, in effect, an all-in-the family entrepreneur, with her father-in-law, Richard Leach, as chairman of the company. Computer software was then—in the early 1980s—in its beginning stage, and educational software was exploding in the schools where the company had its expertise and its principal market. But, DLM was new to the home marketplace.

> *DLM called and said, "We don't know how to build distribution for the home market, but we think you can figure it out. So, if you want the job you have to make your own job description. You have to come up with the whole plan because no one's ever done that before in our company." I had to research the computer software industry quickly and figure out how products were sold and by whom and for how much and what the margins were. I had to build distribution from scratch and organize sales. That helped me tremendously when I had the idea for Barney. It was my salvation, since I had already built sales, marketing and distribution once before.*
>
> *I quickly ordered the trade magazines and studied who was who in the industry . . . what were the*

leading companies . . . what was the retail situation . . . which distributors carried computer software for the home market . . . were chains involved or was business done mainly in independent stores . . . who supplied products to the stores? I called the stores directly and talked to distributors and other people in the software business. I learned that there were probably five distributors in the nation for computer software and usually those distributors were the same ones that distributed books and records to stores.

When we went to market, we did very well. We were in a top position on the best seller charts in those early days and I was able to build national distribution. We had products in all the stores that sold computer software and were in the top five in computer titles for five years running.

When I was sitting on the freeway and had the idea, it was like there were pieces of a puzzle floating around and the pieces suddenly zoomed into place. . . . I had that feeling that all I had to do was connect the dots and eventually the property—the idea— would be realized.

After the software success, Sheryl and her husband Jim moved back to Texas, where he took over as head of a new printing operation at DLM and Sheryl concentrated on taking care of their newborn son. But she didn't stop thinking while she was parenting. Actually, Barney was the third of three entrepreneurial ideas that came out of her life as mother of a small child.

The first idea I had was a baby food product that was packaged in an entirely new way. Baby food is still sold in heavy jars and I came up with an idea for changing that. I made a presentation to Heinz baby food and they liked the idea. But the people at the meeting were laid off a week or so later. Being busy with a small child and having to start all over with selling the idea, I put it aside, though I still may pursue it some day.

The second idea is a bath mat—for which I have three different patents and two manufacturers interested. The mat drapes over the edge of the tub when you bathe a baby. It has small suction cups that hold it to the bathtub and is padded to cushion the ribs when a parent leans over and to protect babies if they stand up and fall against the edge of the tub. The bath mat has a colorful graphic and a netting to hold toys. So for the baby it's a toy and for the parent a safety device that provides comfort and convenience.

The goal was very clear from the beginning: that someday Barney would be known worldwide and would make a positive difference in our world by making a positive difference in the lives of children. . . . It is possible to come up with an idea out of nowhere and to cause it to happen, to go worldwide. . . .

One of the reasons I went ahead with my third idea—for a video—was that my father-in-law had just built a video facility in the printing company and was

> *starting to do videos. Our family business had ware-*
> *houses and an infrastructure into which the idea*
> *could fit. I didn't know anything about making a video*
> *or about production, but I thought, "How hard could it*
> *be [?] I could come up with the story line and then hire*
> *people who know how to produce a video."*

Sheryl phoned her father-in-law, who immediately believed in the idea. He already believed in Sheryl, who had established a track record in turning DLM's educational software into a company winner. He encouraged her to develop her idea and to prepare a presentation for the heads of the company's various divisions to find a taker. That's just what she proceeded to do, true to her entrepreneurial formula of *demand-product-belief.* It was an encouraging experience.

> *What I have found—which could help other entrepre-*
> *neurs—is that when you have an idea and believe in*
> *it, it's almost like the whole world conspires to help*
> *you. Other people want to help you. An extraordinary*
> *chain of events starts to happen. When you need infor-*
> *mation, you open a book and there it is. Or a flyer hits*
> *your desk or you're talking to someone on the phone*
> *and the very information you need is presented. It's*
> *just uncanny. When we needed research information,*
> *it was abundant. It was everywhere. Maybe it's there*
> *all the time and it just runs by you. But when you're*
> *tuning in on an idea, you begin noticing. One statistic*
> *stuck out with us. It was reported at a toy fair in 1988.*
> *Research showed that 39 percent of all money spent*
> *on toys for children up to the age of 18 was spent in*
> *one single year—when the child is two years old!*

Sheryl spent several weeks interviewing store owners and publishing companies, analyzing VCR penetration, and collecting marketing information. She also came up with a story line and had an artist friend illustrate three different stories. Then the unexpected happened to test Sheryl's belief in her idea.

I made a two-hour presentation to the heads of the company's various divisions. They listened and they were very respectful and encouraging and polite. When I was through, they said that they would consider the idea and get back to me. I left assuming that I had succeeded with the presentation. Not at all. They discussed the idea among themselves and decided not to pursue it with me for what they identified as several solid reasons: my idea was not budgeted, none of us really had expertise in how to do it and they felt it would be very difficult to go up against the big publishing companies and big studios that controlled distribution of home videos. They felt that it was going to be impossible for someone from Texas, someone with a new home video, someone from nowhere to build distribution amongst the giants. So they turned it down.

When my father-in-law called to tell me they had turned it down, I just couldn't believe it. When I was sitting on the freeway and had the idea, it was like there were pieces of a puzzle floating around and the pieces suddenly zoomed into place. I had a glimpse of the puzzle completed and how it would be and how it would look when totally completed. I had that feeling that all I had to do was connect the dots and eventually the property—the idea—would be realized. It was so clear to me that if we did it right, it would be unique and there was nothing on the market that was really totally targeted to that age group.

My thinking was different from that of Sesame Street, which was written on two levels. Sesame Street's goal in the beginning was to appeal to adults first and to children second. Their theory was that adults controlled the television dial and they wanted the adults to like it so that they would keep the television tuned to the program. Then their children would watch and learn the educational concepts imbedded in the programs. My thinking was that there is nothing more powerful in the universe than a two-year-old child, who not only controls the dial, but controls the entire household at that age and moment in time. So instead of making something that was just 50 percent targeted to the child and 50 percent targeted to the adult, my idea would be more powerful if it was 100 percent developed and targeted to the child and only to the child.

Sheryl had a financial supporter in her father-in-law. He came to the rescue by investing personally in her video project. His offer was financing to cover the production costs and initial marketing. But, no free ride—after start-up, Sheryl had to make it on her entrepreneurial own. To produce the first videos, she followed through on her initial goal of hiring talent with know-how. She enlisted Dennis DeShazer, who was already a salaried TV producer at DLM, and took on board Kathy Parker, a fellow freelancer with a background in education. They started out as a team of three with input from Sheryl's father-in-law, who added a major asset to his business acumen: "He's a very creative person."

Buried in the development stage, there is a secret about Barney's past worthy of a trivia question, but also an example of how entrepreneurial ideas evolve as they develop into a marketplace product.

In my original plan, Barney was a teddy bear. One of the things that children have always loved is a snuggly. They carry around a blanket or a teddy bear or whatever. What if the thing that is most loved by a child as a snuggly came to life and sang, danced and played with him or her? Like a real friend. At the end of the show it would go back to its snuggly size. I thought that from the eyes of a two-year-old it would be great. So in the beginning days, it was my idea that Barney would be a teddy bear who came to life and played with the kids and then went back down to teddy bear size. As our team formed—with Dennis and Kathy—we kicked around ideas and the video series started fleshing out. At one point, I took my son to a traveling dinosaurs exhibit and he fell in love with dinosaurs. As a teacher, I already knew that kids had always loved dinosaurs. It isn't just a trend or just a fad. It's a classic. So I thought if that's the case, why not make the snuggly a dinosaur? So that's how Barney became a dinosaur.

. . . I think the entrepreneur mentality is the way of the future . . . more and more people are yearning for flexibility and freedom. . . .

My little boy loved Tyrannosaurus Rex, whom we wanted to be friendly. Therefore the smile, big friendly eyes, no claws, no sharp teeth. We wanted him round because round is interpreted as friendly by children. We wanted him big because dinosaurs are big. We made him purple because purple works well with both boys and girls and we added the spots to spice him up a little bit and the green tummy for a warm touch. That's how Barney got to be Barney.

Appropriately, young mothers helped Barney get his start toward becoming what Sheryl describes as a "phe-

nomenon for the pre-school set analogous to Elvis Pres-
ley." She and Kathy Parker recruited neighborhood mothers, called *Mom Blitzers*, in a well-planned marketing
strategy that's a model for entrepreneurial start-ups. It
was shoestring, grassroots marketing (in pre-Internet
times). The *Mom Blitzers* started by selling videos to toy
and video stores—in person and by phone. To expand
awareness of the videos, Sheryl came up with the strategy
of sending copies to preschool and day care centers that
were located near video and toy stores. Her team called it
"Operation Preschool," a two-step process that created a
Barney contagion. Barney won over the fans that
counted—preschoolers—and their parents were not far
behind at the checkout counter in nearby video and toy
stores. Sheryl combined belief in her product with targeted shoestring marketing.

> *All of us were moms, we all had small children and
> we all believed in what we were doing. We believed in
> the video—about the need for it and about the
> demand for it. The goal was very clear from the begin-
> ning: that someday Barney would be known world-
> wide and would make a positive difference in our
> world by making a positive difference in the lives of
> children. That was the goal, that we could somehow
> make a positive difference in our world and show that
> it is possible to come up with an idea out of nowhere
> and to cause it to happen, to go worldwide and make
> a positive difference in the world. It's unbelievable. It
> really is possible.*
>
> *It's amazing what you can do by mail and phone.
> We did telemarketing by buying a list of stores with
> their phone numbers. I trained the mothers in how to
> do telemarketing—as if I knew, I'd never done it—but
> it's just common sense. We would call up these stores
> and tell them about this new video and why as moth-
> ers we thought it was good. We told them that if the*

videos didn't sell that they could send them back. They would order them and we would ship the videos out. Our first videos were priced at $19.95 retail and we would sell them to the store for half of that. It's called "keystoning"—retail selling by the stores at double the cost to them. In those days, the videos cost about $3.50 to reproduce. That cost has come down and so has the retail price, but the keystoning formula is still the same.

Next, a four-year-old video fan opened the door to television for Barney. Little Leora Rifkin in Prospect, Connecticut, fell in love with Barney when her parents bought one of his videos. Her father, Larry, watched with fascination as his daughter played the video again and again, singing and dancing along with the smiling dinosaur. He also happened to be executive vice president of programming for Connecticut Public Television at a time when the Corporation for Public Broadcasting (CPB) and Public Broadcasting Service (PBS) were searching for new quality children's programs. He contacted Sheryl and the Barney team who joined forces with PBS to produce the first 20 TV episodes of *Barney & Friends.* Her team of 10 people worked in a small, rudimentary set to put together the first 20 episodes of what would become the No. 1–rated preschool series on public television.

The Barney Fan Club, which began in 1989 and has registered more than a million members, was overwhelmed with enthusiastic phone calls from parents who told the same story, as reported by *KIDSCREEN Magazine:* "Preschoolers singing, dancing, imagining and learning from the catchy, tuneful episodes in the series. Children were captivated by the lovable purple dinosaur, and parents said they had never seen their children so responsive and excited about a children's program."

Six weeks after his TV debut on April 6, 1992, Barney (and Sheryl) were rocked by a surprise and a setback.

PBS announced that it was withdrawing support for the show and canceling it. But there was no erasing the smile from Barney's face while Sheryl was around. She knew what to do. The grassroots approach that launched the home videos saved the TV show. This time she had a lobbying group at hand in the Barney Fan Club to rally support for the program with a "We Want Barney" campaign. Parents were contacted and urged to get in touch with their local public television stations and demand more Barney episodes. Phone calls to PBS and parents' letters in local newspapers added to the pressure, until Sheryl's campaign succeeded. PBS backtracked; it decided to continue support of *Barney & Friends* episodes and certainly has had no reason for regrets. Eleven million children watch every week a show that in its first three years alone helped to raise more than $15 million for public television from viewers, as well as attract national and local underwriting. (It also has earned seven nominations for the prestigious Emmy Award.)

. . . While sitting in [a] traffic jam, my marketing brain started to kick in. . . . There are millions of parents out there like me and millions of two-year-olds out there like my son. If there could be a product designed specifically for that age group that would hold their attention, something parents felt was good for them as educational, it would be a win-win.

When, 10 years after introducing the Barney home video, Sheryl was one of the producers of *Barney's Great*

Adventure: The Movie, she was reminded of what she had wrought and why Barney works.

> *When Barney arrived on the movie set, the crew was skeptical about filming a big purple dinosaur. Then they grew to see him as something special. I asked them what brought about this change in attitude. They told me it was when they saw the joy and happiness of children when they saw Barney and the unconditional love that Barney brings to them. When you see Barney through a child's eyes, your opinion immediately changes. Barney shows children that anything is possible if you use your imagination and that the gift of imagination and love is powerful. He comes into the child's world and makes them feel safe and special. For me, Barney is an age-less, timeless, wise adult with a child's heart. He believes in innocence and kindness and in the power of imagination. He reaches out to children in their world to underscore their specialness and to encourage them to be the best they can be.*

As carefree as Barney the star appears, Barney the product is subjected to quality controls that match content to audience. The formula is finely tuned, the supporting on-camera cast carefully selected. He is surrounded by Baby Bop, her big brother BJ, and an ethnically diverse cast of children who have fun learning about positive concepts, such as good health and safety habits, friendship, good manners, self-esteem, and concern for others. As part of quality control, Mary Ann Dudko, Ph.D., director of research and development, has a team of educational researchers who work closely with Barney's producers and writers to make sure that Barney leads the way in helping preschoolers enjoy themselves while learning. She identifies his primary attraction as his "nurturing personality and unconditional love, which for a preschool child is very important."

For her part, Sheryl continues to be connected, "almost via umbilical cord," with the many manifestations of Barney: television, film, publishing, licensing, music, radio, "the whole entity, everything that is under the Barney umbrella." She is developing a new animated television series starring BJ, one of the characters in the Barney series (named after B. J. Stamps, Sheryl's father). But there's more underway that's not Barney-bound. She has formed a company, SL Productions, to produce live-action movies; two family-oriented adventure films are already in the works. In addition, she is planning to establish a foundation. Past, present, and future, Sheryl Leach is as enterprising as ever.

> *I'm in a fortunate position in being well-established financially. I'm in a position where I don't have to work, but I still have the same goal. I still want to live life fully and do what I can to make the world a better place. As I do new things, Barney will become one of the things that I have done. I want to enjoy my family and still be very active, to do things like these two movies we're planning. They have exciting plots and very good messages. Whether it's working in Mexico in a mission hospital or in San Antonio at the Literacy Council or in Dallas in the inner city—whatever—they are all forms of trying to make the world a better place.*
>
> *For me, being a woman has always felt good and it's always been a positive thing. It has helped me through all the many things that I have done because I enjoy being a woman. I think people ultimately take their cue from you. As to being an entrepreneur, I think the entrepreneur mentality is the way of the future because more and more people are yearning for flexibility and freedom—which are very important to an entrepreneur. I would encourage women to pursue an idea that comes along if they feel so strongly about it*

that they are willing to focus their time, energy and money on it, if they feel right about it and feel it does something worthwhile.

As for me, when I'm 99 years old and in a rocking chair, I want to look back on my life and feel satisfied that I tried many things, many careers, experienced life fully, learned a lot, loved a lot and did what I could to make the world a better place.

JENNY CRAIG—JENNY CRAIG, INC.

"I've Always Had a Lot of Confidence"

JENNY CRAIG—JENNY CRAIG, INC.
"I've Always Had a Lot of Confidence"

Nearly 40 years ago, Jenny Craig had an experience shared by millions of her weight-loss followers in one way or another. She looked in the mirror and didn't like what she saw: a five-foot-five-inch woman, who had always been slim, was 45 pounds overweight. It had happened, as with so many other weight worriers, gradually. During a difficult pregnancy with her second daughter, her doctor advised her to stay in bed and eat small amounts of food about every half hour. She began with crackers and ginger ale and, by the end of nine months, had graduated to peanut butter and jelly.

Her baby arrived, but the excess pounds remained as Jenny saw another image in that unforgiving mirror: her mother. "My mother was always overweight after having six children. I was the youngest and I never saw her thin. She died when she was only 49 from a stroke. Looking into that mirror, seeing her there in myself, made me realize that if I wanted to live to raise my two daughters, I had to watch my weight." Jenny had plenty of reminders in a family in which weight was a No. 1 health enemy. Her mother had nine brothers and sisters, and eight of them died before the age of 50, all of them overweight.

What Jenny calls her personal *realization* was the beginning of a chain reaction that started with a do-it-yourself solution and led to a weight management colossus: 780 Jenny Craig centers with revenues exceeding $350 million. (Eighty percent of the centers are company owned, 20 percent franchised.) Success took time, experience, self-confidence, risk taking, marketing, and a sense of what people want. First, Jenny got her own weight under control (never deviating thereafter by more than three pounds), then she went to work for fitness clubs—managing, owning, and selling one of her own. After divorcing her first husband and marrying Sid Craig, Jenny partnered with him in setting up meteoric Jenny Craig, Inc. start-ups, first in Australia and then the United States. For Jenny, the entrepreneurial odyssey, with lessons big and small, is rooted in a personal can-do work ethic.

I began to realize that there was nothing out there telling people that they should eat this kind of food as healthy or avoid that kind of food as unhealthy . . . I was sure there were a lot of people just like me that want someone to tell them what to do . . . What really started me off in this business was my own research into what kinds of food I should be eating.

While Jenny was growing up in New Orleans during the Depression, her father transported supplies and crews to oil rigs in the Gulf of Mexico and took on two other jobs to pay the bills for a large family on a tight budget. Along with his example of a hard-work-never-hurt-anyone attitude, he fostered a positive outlook: "He'd always say you can do anything and be anything if you want it enough and I believed him. I've always had a lot of confidence. I think the greatest gift parents can give their kids is a feeling of independence and confidence."

She also remembers the time she was going on a date to the posh Blue Room at the Roosevelt Hotel. It was a daunting prospect for someone whose own parents couldn't afford to go there. "My mother said to me, 'You walk in there like you've been there 100 times before and you own the place.' I did. I have always had that feeling of self-esteem."

It stayed with her. Sid Craig still remembers the impact the mature Jenny made upon him the first time he met her. He had flown in from California to recruit people to staff a fitness center in New Orleans. "The moment I met her I knew she was a top winner. She lit up a room when she came into it. When she attended a training session, she was far superior to the trainer I had sent in. It was obvious she was a gem and, besides that, she was very attractive. She had it all." He also recalls that she had a good figure. At the time, his observation was strictly business: he wanted to hire fitness staffers who looked like they practiced what they preached.

An overweight Jenny had gotten back into shape by joining a gym called Silhouette/American Health. Besides exercising regularly, she cut down on portion sizes, selected her food carefully, and eliminated desserts. She lost unwanted pounds and gained what was then an insight: You must watch what you eat. That's taken for granted today, but not in 1959. "I noticed a need before it was a whole industry and in that sense I was entrepreneurial."

Whoever heard of cholesterol when I first started in this business in 1959? People didn't pay any attention to what they ate. When I grew up in New Orleans my mother was a fabulous Creole cook. Everything we ate involved butter and fat, with lots of starches. I just figured that was the way to eat. It was what I grew up with. Then I read authors like Adele Davis who was considered a kook because she talked about the effect that food had on our overall state of health. I began researching as much as I could and, you know, it's phenomenal to think back to those days. I went to every book store and at most you could buy maybe two or three books that dealt with food and its relationship to health. I began to realize that there was nothing out there telling people that they should eat this kind of food as healthy or avoid that kind of food as unhealthy. That sort of thing. I had to depend on my own research into what kinds of food I should be eating. Back then, when people started talking about eating healthfully, no one wanted to listen—until they started seeing the health risks that were involved. It's like smoking. When they first started talking about the health risk of smoking, people thought that's not going to be me. When I was growing up, probably 80 percent of the people I knew were smoking.

With regard to my own weight problem, I was figuring out what to do. I was always one to exercise. I was already doing that and I wasn't losing weight. I was sure there were a lot of people just like me that want someone to tell them what to do. You'd talk to a doctor and he would just say to eat less. That was the standard reply. Just eat less than you're eating. What really started me off in this business was my own research into what kinds of foods I should be eating.

Not until Jenny's path intersected with Sid's did she put into action the nutritional side of her personal

weight-loss formula and then turn it into weight maintenance. She spent the 1960s working for Silhouette and
learning the business. Having started out as a regular at
the gym, she became interested in people who had lost
weight. She watched them join the gym, arriving "intro-
verted, heads down." If their weight went down, they'd
"come bouncing in. . . . It was a metamorphosis. A person
would change before my eyes." The gym's managers
couldn't help but notice Jenny's strong presence as she
befriended fellow weight losers. They hired her, and soon
she was running the gym. After that, she was running
four other gyms as well—until she made her first entrepreneurial move. She mortgaged her house to raise
enough money to open her own club, Healthetic, which
her drive and know-how made into an immediate success. Jenny then sold it to her former employer and went
on the lookout for a franchise.

Enter 38-year-old Sid Craig, a former dance instructor
and a one-time child tap dancer who was an extra in the
last six *Our Gang Comedies.* While in his senior year at
Fresno State University majoring in business and psychology, Sid taught dancing at night for an Arthur Murray studio. After graduation, he joined the Arthur Murray
Company, where he ended up owning several franchises
and joining the board of directors. His next stop was a
chain of women's fitness salons, which had 17 centers in
California. Sid came on board as a partner to give the
company a jump start by going national with Body Contour, Inc., salons. New Orleans was his first stop to open
a salon, and Jenny was the first person he hired. For her,
the timing was just right.

> *Sid ran an ad in the paper. I had just sold my busi-
> ness and I was looking for a franchise. I thought it
> sounded interesting so I went in to see what it was all
> about. Because a two-year track record was required
> before they would franchise me, they offered me a job*

and I took it. After I became director of the center, Sid and I talked on the phone every day, me in New Orleans, Sid in California. The New Orleans area began to do so well that we expanded from there and pretty soon I was supervising all of the Southern states. Sid called me up one day and asked if I would open Chicago and I agreed to do that. I eventually became national director of operations. At our first national convention which was held in Chicago, Sid asked me where my husband was. I told him I was getting a divorce. He started to smile and said, "That's interesting. So am I." Until then, we had never discussed personal things on the phone. Whenever I talked to him it was strictly business. How many enrollments, how much gross, that kind of stuff.

With both of them free, the inevitable happened. They no longer limited their conversations to business. "We went from being business associates to friends and then lovers," Jenny says. They were married in 1979, having added romance to mutual admiration. Jenny had watched Sid build Body Contours into 200 centers with his unfailing sense for picking the right location and for marketing them. Sid was a fan of Jenny's "enthusiasm and vitality that get people excited about her ideas." He knew they would "make a great team" in business as well as marriage. Jenny's enthusiasm was building for putting into action her nutrition-focused formula for losing weight: "People think of diets as something you go on and off. Ours is a life style." But Jenny's theme of combining exercise and nutrition didn't fly with Sid's partners.

I kept saying to Sid's partners that the world is changing and we really need to start offering more nutritional guidance. But the partners wanted to keep everything status quo. Their attitude was that if something is working, don't change it; if it ain't broke, don't fix it. But you have to keep up with the times. So we gave them three options. Sell to us, buy us out or you take half the centers and we'll take half. Their reply was that they liked things just the way they were. They were totally unreceptive to the options we offered and so the end result was that Body Contour was sold in 1982 to Nutri/System.

. . . Ours was a totally new concept . . . Our dietician told us that Australians would never eat pancakes for breakfast. They ate crepes for lunch . . . [But] once Australians were introduced to pancakes with syrup in the morning it became our biggest seller. It shows you that sometimes you have to go in and try things and not necessarily listen to what the people who are considered knowledgeable tell you.

Because the deal carried a two-year no-compete U.S. clause, the Craigs had to look abroad to carry out their goal of starting a weight-loss company based on Jenny's nutrition-based formula. Australia was their choice. It looked like a Down-Under version of the United States and presented no language barrier. So the Craigs went for broke, using as capital Sid's proceeds from the sale of Body Contour. "We were both fifty when we went to Australia in 1983 and laid everything on the line," Jenny recalls. Sid remembers the doubters who "told us we were nuts," trying to introduce weight-loss centers in a country where the preferred look could be described as "Midwestern beefy." They were warned that Australia was "the toughest market in the world," with 30 paid holidays a year and an understated style that resisted U.S.-style marketing and promotion. They were advised that the United States and Australia are two countries divided by a common language.

Soon after starting up, the Craigs came face-to-face with the Australian difference. At a training class for 100 new staffers, Sid opened the session with a high-energy, upbeat introduction that ended with "And now, here's Jenny."

Silence.

No cheers, not even applause, and certainly not the standing ovation that Sid expected for an opening round in the couple's $1 million start-up investment. Down Under, as the Craigs quickly learned, cheerleading is not in style; understatement is preferred in the land of "Crocodile Dundee."

However, on their side, the Craigs knew what they were doing. Their former company was already in the Australian market and doing well as Gloria Marshall Figure Control Salons. The Craigs were following in successful footsteps and could use the Gloria Marshall track record to identify the most promising places in Australia to set up shop. They started with 12 centers in Melbourne and, by the first year, had expanded to 50. They also took pains to pick a name that would work, as Jenny recalls.

> *We put down about twenty different names on a piece of paper and we talked to every Australian we came in contact with, asking them what they thought would be the best name. Most of the names were generic, things like Ultra-System or New Dimension. Without exception, everyone picked Jenny Craig. When we asked why, they said because we like dealing with a person rather than a corporation.*

Jenny led the way in developing the formula that has become the trademark of Jenny Craig, Inc. The formula is, as summed up by Jenny, "a weight-loss program that involves nutritional guidance, pre-packaged food, exercise and behavior modification." In its fullness, the Jenny Craig formula offers weekly one-on-one counseling sessions; a diet of Jenny's Cuisine, prepackaged foods supplemented by fresh fruits, vegetables, and dairy products; and written and recorded materials, including behavior modification cassettes and suggestions for low-key activity or exercise. To launch operations in Australia, she hired a nutritionist who knew the Australian market and began a hunt for packaged food that met nutritional standards that she had worked out with expert advice and input.

An important lesson to learn is that you're never too old to be successful. I've always thought age is an attitude . . . it just didn't occur to me that age was an obstacle.

To start developing foods, we went to a laboratory and asked them to develop some products. Well, they didn't have any formulas. So they sent us to various food companies. We kept trying the food, tasting and changing the formulas until we finally came up with ten foods, all of them canned. Looking back, they really weren't that good, but it's funny how the mind can rationalize. At the time, I thought they were delicious. I told the companies how much fat we wanted, how much carbohydrates, how much protein. And they devised the recipes from that.

We also had to take into account the fact that the bone structure of Australian women is totally different from that of American women. They have much larger bones so that you can't project Australian women down to a size six. We had to adjust the food formula to Australian women, which we did with the help of the Australian nutritionist we hired.

In Australia at that point, ours was a totally new concept. The country was where we were when I first started in the business 20 years before. There were no comprehensive nutritional programs and the Australians weren't that concerned with how eating relates to health. They always liked fresh fruit, fresh vegetables, but I don't think the motivation was health. I think it was more a matter of taste and a mind set.

It's interesting that we had pancakes on the menu when we first started. It was a mix and all you had to do was add water. Our dietician told us that Australians would never eat pancakes for breakfast. They ate crepes for lunch. So we had her work out a menu that fills pancakes with apples or different fruits to eat as a luncheon dish. Well, to make a long story short, once Australians were introduced to pancakes with syrup in the morning it became our biggest seller. It shows you that sometimes you have to go in and try things and not necessarily listen to what the people who are considered knowledgeable tell you.

Sid, as the quintessential marketer, won national attention for Jenny Craig with his strategy of placing live TV advertisements on Australia's top talent show, "New Faces." The entire country started talking about Jenny Craig, which rapidly achieved the 14th-highest company name recognition. Australians began mentioning Jenny Craig in good-natured wisecracks as the name became synonymous with losing weight and looking good. At one televised international cricket match, the cameras panning the crowd picked up a sign aimed at the overweight captain of the English team: "See Jenny Craig. Quick." The nationwide Australian audience had a good laugh and Jenny Craig centers had a national plug, typical of many others that made the company a household name. Business boomed as Jenny never doubted that it would.

An important lesson to learn is that you're never too old to be successful. I've always thought age is an attitude. I never felt 50 when I went to Australia. I didn't feel any different from the way I felt when I was 35. It just didn't occur to me that age was an obstacle. The nutritionist that we hired when we went to Australia was in her forties and she still to this day says, "I cannot believe that at your age you came over here to a foreign country and started a whole new company." And I say, "Why not?" It didn't occur to me at the time that I was too old or that it wouldn't work. I just knew it would. It's the confidence that I've always had.

Another lesson is to make sure that there's a market for your product or service before you venture into anything. To go into a business and not even know if there's a need out there is suicidal. When we went to Australia, we knew there was a market. We knew that from the Gloria Marshall centers that had succeeded there and we had a whole new concept to add. People think we succeeded overnight, but remember that I had been in the industry since 1959 and I didn't start Jenny Craig until 1983. That's 24 years.

Building a business is like lifting weights. You don't lift a hundred pounds the first day you try. You gradually build up to it. When I started in 1959 there was no way I could have opened Australia or anything like it. You rely on what your past experiences have taught you and you use that to make decisions. You can go on demographics and on recommendations by people who are knowledgeable, but a lot of what you do comes from the gut in making decisions and in hiring people.

When I went to Australia I did all of the interviewing and the training myself. I was like a one-armed paper-hanger working 15 hours a day. I was writing manuals, interviewing and training, working in the centers and helping to prepare the menus. In hiring someone, the Number One thing that I look for is whether they really care about helping someone else. You can teach people the system, but you can't teach them to care. If you talk to them long enough, you spot it. We also had different tests that we gave them. I was asked once what happens if someone doesn't score very high on a test. I said that I go with gut feeling. Our first training class was an example. We had picked a hundred people after interviewing three hundred. After a while we had to select people that we knew wouldn't work out because we needed a hundred so we could open the first 12 centers. I could have told you from the beginning which ones would work out and which wouldn't.

Building a business is like lifting weights. You don't lift a hundred pounds the first day. You gradually build up to it.

Sid adds his firsthand account of Jenny's role in the Australian start-up in which they "combined everything they had learned over the previous 20 years." They started by hiring all the experts they needed in Australia "to put the pieces together," from a nutritionist to a psychologist to a food technologist. "Jenny spearheaded the operation and did most of the writing of the materials. Based on our past experiences, she drew on all the things that were good and eliminated all the bad things." He also shared her confidence. "We both had confidence that by applying our past experience we were going to make it. We never really worried a lot."

> In hiring someone, the number one thing that I look for is whether they really care about helping someone else. You can teach people the system, but you can't teach them to care.

In Australia, their working partnership crystallized. "I am an extreme optimist," Jenny says, "while Sid likes to play the devil's advocate. He wants to know the worst thing that can happen," Jenny says. "I don't even want to think about the worst case. I provide the discipline and stick-to-it-iveness, the elbow grease. Sid is an absolute genius in marketing." Sid also provides the financial know-how that sets centers in motion. "Between my finding locations and doing the marketing and Jenny developing the program and the people to run it, we were both very busy in Australia." It was there that the Craigs established their complementary combination as start-up partners in what Jenny calls a "24-hour job."

I always told people in Australia that I had a 24-hour job because we'd get up in the morning, talk business at breakfast and again at dinner. Our whole life was the business when we were developing the company. Luckily, our kids were grown and on their own, my two daughters and Sid's daughter and two sons. He always tells me that I'm the most unrelenting person he's ever met and it's true. If I make a commitment to something I will stick to it no matter what.

We've always had designated responsibilities. I didn't invade his territory by saying, "Sid, you should be doing this," and he didn't invade mine. I took charge of operations and he was in charge of acquiring all the locations and marketing. We worked hand in hand. I would tell him about the changes that we were making in the field and in operations and ask him what he thought. If he didn't necessarily agree, he'd say that I should consider some other factors or that maybe such and such is a better direction to go. When Sid would say that he was thinking of running a particular ad and I'd say that we should consider how it would play in the field, he'd listen to what I had to say.

The important thing is communications. You have to acknowledge the other person's point of view and feelings. To say something is a stupid idea totally discredits the other person. We like to suggest a different way of looking at the situation. Both Sid and I have good communications skills and because of that we've been able to address issues and differences of opinion in calm, civilized ways.

By 1985, the Australian operation had a gross income of $50 million and was providing $10 million a year for its U.S. parent company. For the entrepreneurial Craigs, who always had planned to return home, the two-year no-compete clause had expired. It was time to start up Jenny Craig in the United States, in familiar territory—California.

We could have lived very comfortably without doing anything else, but we felt we were too young to retire at 52 years old. So we decided to go back to work here in America, back to 12-to-15-hour days. We started up, using the cash generated by the company, the way we've always operated. We didn't take out any loans. Sid feels the way I do—that cash is king. We never borrowed money to expand. We always expanded with the money generated by the business. We always had lines of credit because we learned a long time ago that you can never get a loan when you need it. So if you get a line of credit when you don't need it, it's there if you ever do need it. In a cash business based on service, that's easier to do than with a business where you need inventory. Then you need to borrow for your inventory.

In building our business, word of mouth has always been a major factor. That happens when you've got a good product, provide good service, [and] have good people working for you.

We chose Los Angeles because it was our home and had enough population to justify opening 12 centers in the area. Our timing was good, but as we realized after opening on a Monday with full-page newspaper ads, we had 11 competitors with a foot already in the door. We knew the competition was there, but were surprised at how strong they were in terms of advertising. We realized that we had to do something different. That's when we started researching frozen dinners and found that no other company was offering frozen dinners on the premises. Weight Watchers had frozen dinners in the supermarket, but they were not part of their program.

We looked for a small company that was supplying food to hospitals and it agreed to produce the quantities that we needed. As it turned out, we became their biggest account. Once we started with frozen dinners, we immediately captured interest and it made a huge difference in our business. In those days, the frozen dinners intrigued people, who came in to see what our program could do and then they enrolled.

We also found an interesting phenomenon. The markets where we had the most competition were our best markets. I realized why. There was greater awareness of the risks of obesity and a major reason is the advertising we and all the other companies were doing. As to picking locations, we had the advantage that Sid had lived in Los Angeles and knew the market from his years with Gloria Marshall salons. He knew the best neighborhoods and sections. Here we had a leg up on competitors who go strictly by demographics. We had other ways of identifying locations, a lot of it based on previous experience.

In building our business, word of mouth has always been a major factor. That happens when you've got a good product, provide good service, have good people working for you. People see the advertising and come in. When they achieve success in the program, they bring in their friends. We've always done a huge portion of our business from referrals. I think that most people recommend our program, not because they have anything to gain, but because they really believe in it.

This fits my personal goal to help as many overweight people as possible break that cycle of failed diets. I don't want them to experience the feelings of embarrassment, depression and anxiety that often *accompany being severely overweight. I want to show them how to turn despair into victory.*

Five years after entering the U.S. marketplace, the company became the sixth-fastest-growing private firm in the country. Jenny identifies the company's emphasis on finding, hiring, and training quality staffers as crucial to the U.S. success—from 12 Los Angeles centers in 1985 to almost 800 in 1998, located in Australia, New Zealand, and Puerto Rico, as well as the United States. "Good people are key," she says, citing her best sources of personnel: former nurses and teachers and graduates of college programs in nutrition and psychology. Teachers, in particular, provide a Jenny Craig combination of talents— good communication skills, ability to get information across, and empathy. She's convinced that the kind of people she hires differentiates Jenny Craig, Inc., from the competition. When she hires someone, she wants to find out whether they "really care about helping people or are they just looking for a job."

On the product side, the centers offer an exclusive line of Jenny Craig foods, 70 different products that include fresh frozen complete meals for menus based on U.S. government guidelines. The cuisine, which accounts for more than 90 percent of company sales, ranges from popcorn and peanut butter bars to banana bran muffins and bagel chips. The main dishes combine international dishes—chicken cacciatore, chicken enchilada, teriyaki steak—with standards like baked turkey and macaroni and cheese

Jenny and Sid have no doubt that the need and the market are there for what they offer. They point to the statistics. Obesity is widespread and increasing. U.S. government estimates in 1997 showed that 35 percent of the adult population is clinically obese, their numbers increasing by 10 percent since 1980. Obesity is characterized by many health experts as the most common chronic disease in the United States. It is linked to 5 of the 10 leading causes of premature death. Only smoking kills more people. Even small amounts of weight loss—10 to 15 percent of initial body weight—can have significant health benefits for people suffering from obesity.

In the nationwide fight against fat, Jenny Craig, Inc., has gone all out to promote Jenny's antifat formula. At its 15-year milestone, the company reported that it had spent more than one-half billion dollars to promote Jenny Craig's message and noted in its annual report that "the Jenny Craig brand has never been stronger." Advertising has played a major role in spreading the message, notably TV commercials that have tracked the weight loss of celebrities as well as ordinary clients. The ads are backed up by best-selling Jenny Craig cookbooks (*The Jenny Craig Cookbook* and *No Diet Required*), various written materials, and audio- and videocassettes.

The 1990s presented new challenges for the company in the face of increasing competition, a 1993 hassle with the Federal Trade Commission about advertising (settled in 1997 with a consent agreement), and fiscal pressures stemming from a downturn in the weight-loss industry. But that's yesterday's news in a company in which Jenny and Sid are unyielding in their look-ahead, upbeat style of doing business.

The company was restructured in the mid-1990s and its approach updated. In response to changing times and changing conditions for their time-pressured customers, Jenny Craig introduced in August 1997 a user-friendly ABC Program that emphasizes convenience and simplicity. It replaces lengthy workbooks and structured menu plans with a short, interactive pocketbook guide and a flexible menu plan for making daily choices from an A, B, or C category, without needing to calculate calories or fat grams. It also places greater emphasis on the hardest time in losing weight—the first few weeks—while continuing to emphasize a combination of nutrition, physical activity, and behavioral changes. As far as Jenny is concerned: "Life should be enjoyed, not wasted counting fat grams and calories. That's the beauty of the ABC Program. It makes a healthy lifestyle as easy as A-B-C."

As another sign of keeping up with the times, Jenny Craig, Inc., is exploring development of virtual centers on the Internet where food can be ordered instead of going to a center. In areas where there are no Jenny Craig centers, customers can call Jenny Direct on an 800 number for a home program. Then, there's the demand for the Jenny Craig label in the current age of branding. Vitamins and exercise equipment head the list of prospects, not to mention requests that range from leotard and shoe manufacturers to a French company that even wants to label its product as "Lean and Thin Water."

In talking of expansion, Jenny talks of "things on the drawing board that are going to be as exciting as it was in the beginning for the company." Whatever emerges will have one predictable characteristic that goes back to the way Jenny Craig started with her own do-it-yourself program and her first experiences with fellow weight worriers in a New Orleans gym: "self improvement."

3

RUTH FERTEL—
RUTH'S CHRIS STEAK HOUSE

"Treat Others the Way You Want to Be Treated"

3

RUTH FERTEL— RUTH'S CHRIS STEAK HOUSE

"Treat Others the Way You Want to Be Treated"

In the kitchen of a New Orleans steak house, a five-foot-two-inch, 110-pound former lab technician was picking up 30-pound slabs of beef, sawing the bone by hand, and cutting up USDA Prime steaks. After each slab, she was so exhausted that she collapsed for a half hour on a mattress in a back room, then was up again, greeting customers, helping the restaurant's three waitresses, and doing the books in the middle of the dining area—until it was time to cut more steaks.

Out front, patrons at lunch and dinner had a choice of steak or steak—filets, New York strips, and rib eyes, and a choice of two salads. No menu. The waitresses rattled off the limited à la carte choices. Steaks were $5. With salad, potatoes, dessert, and coffee, a meal ran $7 or $8. The place was then called Chris Steak House. The year was 1965. The meat cutter and steak house owner was Ruth Fertel, who at the time probably knew no more about running a restaurant than her 35 diners a day.

There are two contrasting recollections Ruth Fertel has about that beginning of what has become America's largest upscale restaurant company, Ruth's Chris Steak House.

> *The restaurant staff was expecting me to fail, just like the others who had bought the restaurant before me, especially since I was a woman.*
> *Actually, I never had a doubt that I would make it.*

The skepticism and the certainty were focused on a 17-table, 60-seat steak house on North Broad Street, 20 blocks from downtown New Orleans. No matter how confident she was, Ruth could never have envisioned the outcome, 33 years later: Ruth's upscale, millionaire-generating chain of 66 restaurants (franchised and company-owned) that are serving 15,000 steaks a day and grossing $230 million a year as the largest upscale restaurant company in the United States.

Neither Ruth's close friend and attorney, nor the president of the bank he owned, would ever have bet that Ruth would have made it in the first place in one small steak house. Their advice was straightforward: *Don't buy it.* If she had done due diligence, even she might have had second thoughts, but like many other entrepreneurs, she refused to be deterred. As to experience, she was earning $4,800 a year as a lab technician at Tulane Medical School, a respectable income at the time for a working woman, but a job that had nothing to do with owning a business.

> *I was looking for a business to go into. I was divorced, alone, and I had two boys, 15 and 16, who would soon be going to college and I was not making enough money at Tulane. So I began searching through the ads for business opportunities in the daily paper. I didn't know where else to look. I was so naive. I didn't have any special interests besides hunting, fishing and reading and it didn't sound like I could make*

much money out of any of them. I saw lots of ads for service stations, but that wasn't for me. Neither were the bars that were listed.

Then after seeing an ad for Chris Steak House, I said to myself, "Simple menu. I know I can do that!" I had eaten there. The food was really good and it had a great reputation. So I went to the restaurant and met with the owner. I asked him, "How much do you want?" He said, $18,000 and I said I would buy it. I didn't have any money, but I had my home. In talking to him, I asked him when he went into business for the first time and he told me February 5, 1927. I said, "You've gotta be kidding. That was the exact day I was born." What an omen! I knew I was going to make a success out of that business. I went to my bank, which was owned by my attorney and good friend. His name is Scott. He sent me to his bank president to negotiate a loan with my house as collateral. Both advised me against buying the restaurant. They really talked against it, particularly Scott. He warned me that I would lose my house.

The bank president said that he'd lend me the money because I had my house as collateral. I had gotten it in the divorce. "Ruth," he said, "I'll lend you the money because you want it and you've got the collateral, but I strongly advise against it." To show you how naive I was at the time, I was ready to borrow only the $18,000 required to buy the restaurant, but the bank president pointed out that I needed to borrow an additional $4,000 so I could buy food and supplies!"

That's not all. Scott visited the restaurant after he knew I wanted to buy it and then called me to say, "Ruth, they have a sign up saying they're going out of business." I said, "Oh Lord." So we rushed the actual sale so that it would take place two days later—on May 24. After everything was signed, the former *owner came in, showed me around and showed me what to do. Then he emptied the cash register and left, even though he was supposed to stay around for a few weeks to show me how to run the business. In particular, he was supposed to show me how to butcher the meat, which he only showed me once— that one time right before the sale. Cutting the meat was something he always did himself. No one of the four people on the kitchen staff ever did it.*

I was looking for a business to go into. . . . I began searching through the ads for business opportunities in the daily paper. I didn't know where else to look. I was so naive. I didn't have any special interests. . . . Then after seeing an ad for Chris Steak House, I said to myself, "Simple menu. I know I can do that!"

Meanwhile, meat had never been that expensive and he advised me to buy from the supplier who provided the better meat while he himself was serving both prime and choice. He served prime to the customers he knew and choice to those he didn't. Even after finding out what he was doing, I never mixed the meat. I always served only prime and still do. Over time, I learned something else. I was only one of a string of buyers for the restaurant. I was the seventh and the others had either failed or they gave up because of the long hours. Each time, Chris would start up the restaurant again and sell it again. He made more money restarting and selling than running it.

Since no one else knew how to butcher the 30-pound loins, I had to do it myself from the first day. I was told that butchering with a hand saw was the only way to do it and that's the way I did it for the first two weeks. But it was just too much. So I bought an electric saw. All the stores butcher their meat with electric saws and once I switched, it became much easier. But I was still lifting and butchering 30-pound loins. After five years, I developed a really bad case of bursitis in my elbows and had to stop. That's when I started teaching my people how to butcher. But I was still doing the bookkeeping and the reservations and seating people and whatever else was necessary. If the dishwasher didn't show up, I did the dishes. On Mondays, which was the chef's day off, I did the cooking—for 12 hours, from 11:30 to 11:30.

What happened almost immediately overwhelmed conventional wisdom and justified her entrepreneurial confidence. She made money. In the first six months, she cleared more than double her previous annual salary. She also discovered how tough the restaurant business is, working from 9:00 A.M. until all diners left at 1:00 or 2:00 the next morning. For all purposes, she was *living* at the restaurant. Meanwhile, her on-site presence and her customer-friendly way of running the restaurant were having an impact, as they always do in service-intensive businesses. Her customers were feeling at home in her restaurant. At night, they'd stay from two to three hours, never feeling pressured to leave. It came to be said that when you come to her restaurant, "you buy the table."

She developed a business formula that was on target for her chosen industry, doing what successful entrepreneurs do. They figure out—whether by instinct or design—what the particular marketplace wants and what will draw customers. For the restaurant industry, her formula was a combination of a quality product—only USDA

Prime—and service—Southern hospitality that became a magnet for diners. Ruth speculates that there were "other things I should have known, but I understood that customers wanted good food and they wanted to be treated well. . . . In the end, that's what all of this is based on." The hospitality part came naturally.

> *My mother was a great, great hostess. She made everyone feel so welcome in her home. She lived by the golden rule, "Treat Others the Way You Want to Be Treated," and she instilled it in my brother and me. In the restaurant, I wanted to make people feel comfortable and treat them as if they were guests in my home, which is what we did. We went out of our way to please customers. We spoiled them. I'll give you an example. One of our regular Sunday customers was operated on for his teeth and couldn't bite into a steak. So I chopped his steak in the grinder, formed it into the same shape as before and served it to him. He was thrilled. We did things like that to please our customers and they realized that we were trying to make them feel at home, to regard our steak house as their second home. On Saturdays at lunch time some customers who had become friends would come and we'd all cook together. It was great fun for me especially, since I didn't have to do all the cooking.*
>
> *And the business kept growing. At the end of the year, I paid income tax on $9,000, which for me was a lot more than the $400 a month I earned at Tulane. I said—like Jackie Gleason—"How sweet it is."*

At one point, when Ruth was stymied in her attempts to increase lunchtime revenues, she told a devoted patron about her problem. He was an executive with an oil service company who came to lunch regularly, bringing potential customers from area oil companies as guests. Ruth told him that she was thinking of reducing the size of the lunchtime portions as a way of coping with the high cost of quality meat.

> *We always have served extremely large portions and serving small portions was something I didn't want to do even back then. I said to him: "I'm thinking of doing a smaller steak for lunch because I'm just unable to increase my lunch revenues." He said, "You know Ruth, I like this place because we get your undivided attention, but if you want more business, you'll have more business." Well, every day he would bring in a different person. They all liked the restaurant and would come back for dinner as well as lunch. Or if someone wanted to take them out to lunch, they'd say, "Let's go to Chris Steak House." The business really started building mainly because of customers like him.*
>
> *When people came to eat, they could watch me work. I put my desk in the dining room and did my bookkeeping there. If I was butchering, I left the door open. If I was cooking, I left the door open. My customers could see how hard I was working. They felt sympathetic and they loved my product so much that they didn't want me to fail so they helped build my business to keep me in business.*

Ruth had barely mastered the art of carving up and cooking steaks and was just getting accustomed to the long restaurant days when Hurricane Betsy struck, three and a half months after she took over the business. Her response was a lesson in how an entrepreneur's best instincts can turn around adversity. For New Orleans, the hurricane's impact was devastating. For Ruth's steak house, it meant total spoilage when her electricity went down, and she couldn't find any refrigerated storage space that hadn't been rented already. She promptly turned a business disaster into a good deed that increased her visibility and popularity in a city where helping your neighbor counts for a lot. She cooked every-thing she had in the restaurant, particularly the meat, and added whatever else would spoil, creating a substantial food package. Then she called her brother who had a restaurant 50 miles downriver from New Orleans to pick up the food and distribute it to people in his area who had hardly anything to eat. She not only earned appreciation from those who benefitted; she soon discovered that many of them turned up as customers.

When electricity was restored to her restaurant after a week, her mealtimes had a new set of customers in the emergency telephone and utility crews working around the clock to restore service. They were steak eaters, with what seemed to Ruth "an unlimited expense account," and they ate at her restaurant every day. Even the local bishop cooperated in heavily Catholic New Orleans. Because the city was cut off from fish supplies, the bishop gave Catholics a dispensation from what was then a church ban against meat on Friday. It was the one day of the week that the restaurant had been closed, but no longer. Ruth opened on Fridays, which became, along with Saturdays, one of her two best nights. It also meant that the kitchen crew lost that day off. Ruth replaced it with Monday and replaced the chef at the stove, learning firsthand how hot it gets in the kitchen.

> *If you get 20 orders at one time and five are rare, five medium rare, three medium, two medium well, how do you know when each is done? And you're standing there in front of a very hot stove. Our stoves are at 1800 degrees. It's an extremely hot job and I have nothing but praise for these chefs. It's an art, a technique and the only way of learning how to do it is to do it. That's how I learned.*

After Hurricane Betsy, the word spread downtown about Chris Steak House, benefit of the customer grapevine. The lunchtime business executives who brought associates and customers started coming back in the evening with their wives. The word got around to government officials and politicians downtown. They started coming, as did media personalities and sports figures. (The day Mohammed Ali came to eat a well-done porterhouse big enough for two, the police had to be called out within minutes to control the crowd of fans and well-wishers.) The steak house developed the kind of branding that makes restaurants prosper. It became the "in place" in New Orleans, where diners shook hands with friends on the way to their table, and where it was said that all kinds of political and business deals were made. The restaurant became a success built by good steaks and good friends.

In the restaurant, I wanted to make people feel comfortable and treat them as if they were guests in my home, which is what we did. We went out of our way to please customers.

By 1969, the small steak house on North Broad Street could in no way handle the business. Diners waiting for tables were crowded together at the entrance. Many others saw the crowd and gave up. They left. Not only was business lost, but the welcome mat pulled out from under eager diners. For Ruth, "it was a knife turning in my stomach." An immediate solution was a second restaurant across the river in Gretna, Louisiana, which was a center for oil field workers and managers. A close friend teamed up with Ruth to open that restaurant, which was a success as soon as the first steak was served up. The demand still didn't let up, so Ruth opened a third New Orleans restaurant in suburban Metairie.

Ruth makes no secret about what it takes to serve up her much-publicized steaks, starting with a choice of six degrees of doneness for a giant serving of sirloin strip, filets, rib eye, or porterhouse (for two, three, or four persons).

> *First of all, the beef must be corn fed. If it isn't corn fed, it'll be tender, but it won't have any flavor. That means it must come from the Corn Belt, which extends from western Ohio to eastern Nebraska and north-eastern Kansas. We use large portions—12 to 22 ounces—because a larger cut of meat retains its natural juices during cooking. It must be cooked at the right temperature, 1,700 to 1,800 degrees. We only use gas. We don't use charcoal, although I do like charcoal broiled steaks. We use gas to get the full flavor of the beef. Another reason our steaks are so good is—believe it or not—that we add salt and pepper before we cook them. The fire is so hot that it melts the salt and sears the meat very quickly. It becomes crusty and it's wonderful.*
>
> *In New Orleans we've always put a little butter on the steak after it's cooked—whole butter, not drawn butter. The butter is added after the steak is cooked and just before it goes to the table on a plate that's heated to 450 to 500 degrees. The butter melts and sizzles as it drips onto the plate. It's so appetizing, butter and beef just go together. On that plate, the steak is hot from the first to the last bite.*
>
> *These are the secrets of a great steak.*

As Ruth approached the end of her 10-year lease on North Broad Street, she had no doubt about committing to another 10 years, even though her landlord doubled the rent. She didn't particularly like her landlord, to boot, but she had no intention of leaving her corner location that was so well known. Still, as a backup, she had bought a building four blocks down Broad Street and rented it out for weddings, dances, and social affairs so that it paid for itself.

Six months into the new lease, another disaster struck. A fire closed the restaurant, leading to yet another friendly rescue.

> *It seems that every time something bad happened, something good would come from it. First it was the hurricane and business just escalated after that. Then the fire, which made it necessary to move. I remember calling my friend at the bank in a state of shock, crying and telling him what happened. He asked me, "Do you still own that building down the street?" When I said yes, he said, "Look I have a contractor with me right now. We'll get you open in seven days." It was unbelievable. They did it. They fixed up the building as a restaurant and I went from 60 seats to 160. Since then we've enlarged it and it now seats 240. People who were discouraged by the two-hour wait at my first location suddenly started showing up. Business boomed again.*

With the change of location, Ruth had to change the name of her restaurant, because she only had the right to use the name so long as she remained at the original location. Her solution was simple: add Ruth to the name. It salvaged name recognition for those who knew the restaurant, and for those who didn't . . . well, the name is so unusual that it's more or less memorable. (One restaurant critic has commented that Ruth's Chris Steak House is such a tongue twister that it can be used as a sobriety test: anyone who can rattle off the name three times in a row can't be drunk.)

Ruth's next major move—once again—was friendship driven, but not until she overcame her initial hesitation.

In 1976, one of my most loyal customers, T. J. Moran, moved to Baton Rouge, which is about 80 miles north of New Orleans. Every time he wanted a steak he would drive here to have one and he always liked to have drinks with his meal. Finally, he said to me, "Ruth, every time I want a good steak, I come here, but I can't drink because I have to drive back to Baton Rouge. You've got to let me open one of your restaurants in Baton Rouge." I said, "No, I can't do that."

He was coming down three or four times a week trying to talk me into it until finally I agreed. We went to an attorney and signed a franchise agreement. Then I saw the location for the new restaurant. It wasn't actually in Baton Rouge, but 20 miles outside. I told him that people might drive out at night for dinner, but I didn't see that he would have much lunch business. Little did I take into account that there were oil refineries nearby up and down the river. It turned out that he was busier at lunch than at dinner. Of course, it was the same menu as I had and the restaurant was a success from the very beginning.

T. J. Moran recalls what it was like to be a regular customer and then a franchisee. Eating at the original restaurant was like going to a private club: "You saw the same guys every day for lunch, particularly the ones who did a lot of lunch entertaining. It's interesting. There was an equally good steak house right across the street, but it didn't have the same energy as Ruth's place where it was fun to be and where you felt special and privileged. It was like being invited to her home." As a friend and as Ruth's largest franchisee (with seven restaurants), he has experienced her as the "most loyal person he has ever known," and someone who was "very, very helpful," once she gave in and agreed to franchising. "She's not someone who dwells on setbacks. She's always going forward."

Once Ruth said yes to T.J.'s franchise, she went in two directions, opening her own restaurants and making franchise agreements—starting with two franchises in Houston and a company restaurant in Lafayette, Louisiana. It was a calculated strategy. Steak is a standard businessperson's meal, particularly when on the road. In Ruth's restaurant, the same high standard could be relied upon while the decor varied from one location to another. People involved in the oil industry went back and forth among her various cities and would welcome the sight of another Ruth steak house. They were also a ready-made grapevine to pass the word around.

As with all expansions, quality control is a major issue, one that Ruth personally resolved. She spent three weeks at each new restaurant teaching the cooking staff the recipes and training them in her distinctive way of cooking everything, particularly steaks. While she had confidence in the entrepreneurial skills of her franchisees, she also made certain that their staffers fulfilled the hospitality half of her restaurant formula. So she sent her own staffers to train them. The results have been consistently impressive for the company and for the franchisees who have become millionaires themselves.

> When I started franchising, that really got the name out and the more the name became known, the busier we became in all our restaurants. Our name recognition spread. In fact, all our franchisees were people who had eaten at one time or another in one of our restaurants. We never looked for franchisees. They came to us. We have 42 franchises, but they are owned by only 17 franchisees. In all our restaurants, people know what to expect—the same great service and hospitality. Our menus are practically the same, though we may have an item or two in different locations because certain dishes are popular there. We

have 66 different looks so that people feel they're at a different restaurant, but they know what they're going to get—great steaks. In New Orleans, if visitors eat sea food for two or three nights, they say, "Oh, my Lord, I need a piece of meat." If they find me on the first night, they'll eat here every night for two, three, four nights in a row.

I put my desk in the dining room and did my bookkeeping there. . . . If I was cooking, I left the door open [so] my customers could see how hard I was working. They felt sympathetic and they loved my product so much that they didn't want me to fail. . . .

You know one of my favorite sayings is that people talk a better game than they play. When we opened a restaurant in Beverly Hills, people said we were absolutely crazy to go to California. They don't eat meat in California. Well, let me tell you that they eat a lot of meat in California. In addition to Beverly Hills, we now have restaurants in San Diego, Irvine, Palm Desert and San Francisco and they're among our busiest restaurants.

Ruth, who considers herself "lucky to fall into a business that I love," turned the tables on the banking profession by convincing a banker to become a restaurateur. She advised a close friend, Leona Clade, who was a bank officer: "If you want to make money instead of having your name on a desk, then go into the restaurant business." Leona took the advice. She bought an Italian restaurant and signed a five-year lease. Only when Leona went to negotiate a second five-year lease did she learn that Ruth had silently co-signed the lease and guaranteed it. (Leona calls it Ruth's style—a helping hand that leaves no fingerprints.) Another five years in her Italian restaurant and Leona was ready to open a Ruth's Chris Steak House in Dallas in 1981 (her second franchise was opened in 1986). As far as she's concerned, if you follow Ruth's guidelines, you "can't help but succeed." You provide first-quality food, hospitality, and good service, and you'll make it. In raving about Ruth as sensitive, caring, determined, and also someone who knows how to make the tough decisions, Leona finally gets stuck for words and settles for "She's special," then adds, "When I grow up, I want to be Ruth Fertel!"

When I started franchising, that really got the name out and the more the name became known, the busier we became in all our restaurants. . . . In fact, all our franchisees were people who had eaten at one time or another in one of our restaurants.

Lana Duke, whose public relations and advertising agency has served Ruth since 1976, also became a franchisee, first in San Antonio and next in Toronto. No one has been in closer contact with Ruth over the years of her rapid expansion. "Entrepreneurs can get in a slump when they procrastinate in pursuing a goal," Lana comments. "Ever since I've known Ruth, when she decides to do something she does it, day after day after day. She never procrastinates. She stays focused."

As an entrepreneur, Ruth identifies *focus* as the key. "I've always operated on the KISS principle—keep it simple, stupid." Actually, her success as entrepreneur involves much more. It demonstrates how entrepreneurs are made rather than born. What has counted is her combination of training, skills, and personal traits that are success factors in any industry. The better the match between such a combination and the circumstances the better the odds for success, but the key traits of sound judgment, determination, hard work, and the capacity to keep learning make a difference in any business. An industry provides the opportunity. Timing improves the odds. But it's up to the entrepreneur to turn opportunity to success.

Ruth, for all her gentle demeanor and unassuming style, is a strong-willed businessperson. Her vice president for marketing and public relations, Harry Day, describes her as the most competitive person he's ever met: "In everything she does she has a goal in mind. Don't get in her way once she starts. But she is also very nice, genuinely nice. She knows that you don't have to be ruthless to succeed." Ruth's competitive spirit developed while growing up in the Mississippi Delta–backwater town of Happy Jack, Louisiana, with a hard-driving father who sold insurance and a mother who taught kindergarten. Ruth describes herself as "always trying to do as well as the boys did."

At 15, she graduated from high school and headed to Louisiana State University where she graduated at 19, a chemistry and physics major. Her favorite subject was math, which, she found, "teaches you to think logically." She stayed on for a master's degree, but cut that short because she "couldn't stand school any more." She also quit a short-lived teaching job at McNeese Junior College in Lake Charles, Louisiana, where she had to deal with students her age or older. It turned out that she hated teaching: "When I got to the point where I hated to go to work in the morning, I knew it wasn't for me. After teaching summer school I left, got married, and had two children."

My staff taught me a whole lot, since I'd never been in the restaurant business before. Ever since, I've always hired people that know more than I do.

Her one early venture into entrepreneuring came soon after her divorce. The venture originated at her bridge club when she started making drapes with three other women for another member. One woman said, "The drapes are so beautiful. You could sew for people." Ruth's reaction was, "I'm in business." The next day she put an ad in the local newspaper and the orders flowed in. She soon was earning $1,000 a month, which made a major difference to a mother with two teenage sons trying to get along on $300-a-month alimony. Ruth sewed the drapes by hand, spreading them out on the living room floor and working away on her hands and knees. But her knees gave out, forcing her to give up drapery making and look for a job.

I went to a local supermarket and applied for a position as a cashier or whatever. The manager had me fill out an application and after he read it he said I was overqualified for the job so he wouldn't even hire me. I was devastated. I went home and cried. That's when I went to an employment agency and got the job at Tulane in the cardiovascular, radioactive research lab. The job was fun because my immediate superior was a doctor who did a lot of experiments. But I reached a

point where I wasn't earning enough, forcing the deci-
sion to go into business for myself.

Her own flashback to the first days in business as a steak house owner demonstrates that for entrepreneurs it need not be how much they know but how much they can learn. In 1997, *Restaurants & Institutions* magazine named Ruth Fertel "Executive of the Year." In 1965, she couldn't even get drink orders straight.

> *When I began in the steak house, I asked the wait-*
> *resses what I could do. They said that after I seated*
> *people, take the drink order and they'd take it from*
> *there. I said, "Okay, that sounds simple." After the first*
> *drink orders I took, I'd come back to them and admit—*
> *because I'm not a drinker—that I couldn't remember*
> *what the customers wanted. So they took that job*
> *away from me. It was kind of a comedy of errors in the*
> *beginning because I was learning as I went along. My*
> *staff taught me a whole lot, since I'd never been in the*
> *restaurant business before. Ever since, I've always*
> *hired people that know more than I do.*

In 1997, she went out and hired William Hyde, Jr., the president of her chief competitor, Morton's Restaurant Group, who marvels at her success (once as a competitor, then as a collaborator), prospering 33 years in a segment of the restaurant industry that is male dominated and "where many a great company and many a great entrepreneur have fallen by the wayside." How has she done it? "By downright perseverance and determination. She doesn't surrender. She doesn't back off. She stays focused. She persists. She'll bend, but she won't break. She's a true entrepreneur. She knows that there's no reward without risk."

For anyone who wants to be an entrepreneur, Ruth has three pieces of advice: "One, love what you do. Don't go into a business where every day of work is a chore. You won't enjoy it, the people around you won't enjoy it, and it's very hard to be successful in something you don't love. Second, expect to work hard and to work long hours. Whenever you work for yourself, you work twice as hard as you ever would for somebody else. So expect to put the time in to be successful. Third, stay focused on your business and, most importantly, stay focused on your customers. Know what they want. Listen to them, and when they make a suggestion, respond to it."

As for Ruth Fertel herself, she shows no signs of letting up. As company chairman, she works closely with CEO Hyde to monitor current operations, review strategy, and make plans for the future. She is continuously on the phone with her managers and franchisees to see how they're doing and to provide any help they need. In 1997, she personally visited 42 of her restaurants to "smell out how they're doing." She's already serving steaks in 28 states, as well as Washington, D.C., Puerto Rico, Taiwan, Hong Kong, Mexico, and Toronto, Canada. Her plans call for more company-owned restaurants rather than franchises, opening at the rate of four to five a year for several years and expanding to between 100 and 120 different locations. In all this, she views herself "not so much as a restaurateur as a businessperson"—with no intention of stopping.

> *I always live in the present and the future, never in the past. We're growing and will continue to grow. That's the fun and has always been the fun. We're going to open more and more restaurants, always keeping my good name. I never want that to suffer. I want us to get better and better and better.*

Joy Mangano—
Ingenious Designs, Inc.

"The Product Is Always King"

Joy Mangano—
Ingenious Designs, Inc.

"The Product Is Always King"

Millions of mops were at stake when Joy Mangano faced the home shopping management of QVC and heard the ultimate put-down for her invention, the Miracle Mop: "Nobody wants to buy this mop."

The management team didn't take into account that they were face-to-face with boundless belief and determination in an entrepreneur who maintains, "You have to believe in your products and you have to be determined. If one avenue doesn't work, you find another one."

With all the conviction that has since made her a Pied Piper in the booming marketplace of home shopping television, she said, "Just let *me* get on TV with it and I'll show you what an exciting product it is."

Everyone around the conference table had agreed that the Miracle Mop wasn't selling up to QVC's requirements—the product that Joy had not only invented, but also manufactured and marketed as the "original cotton, self-wringing mop with the machine washable, bleachable, replaceable head," as "literally the last mop you'll ever have to buy." In retrospect, the last-minute opportunity she pushed for and won that afternoon late in 1992 was probably the most important sale she has ever made and certainly one that she can never forget.

> *I came in to meet with QVC to discuss where my prod-ucts were going on TV and was told that they wanted to return the Miracle Mop. It wasn't selling at the rate per minute that products have to sell on home shopping TV. Everyone in the room was agreeing that it should go back, what they call in the trade, "Return to Vendor." As far as I was concerned, QVC wasn't demonstrating the product properly. They were showing stills of the mop and they really didn't know the product. It just wasn't clicking. There wasn't any chemistry.*

Don't let anyone tell you that you can't take one small step at a time in the beginning. I hired my first produc-tion employee from a local church with the cooperation of the pastor, who put up a Help Wanted sign.

> *I was saying to myself that I know they're wrong. This is a great product. I knew that it would sell if I demonstrated it. So I said to them, "Let me get on TV with it and I'll show you what an exciting product it is." It took one executive there, one very bright man— Doug Briggs, who is now president of QVC—to say, "Fine, we'll give you one opportunity to sell it." I knew there and then that the whole future for Miracle Mop depended on this opportunity and I can tell you I was very, very nervous.*
> *I had absolutely nothing memorized when I went live on QVC, but I had demonstrated the mop in*

stores, in boat shows, in fairs and in places like that and had already talked about the great benefits of the product—though never before on TV. When my turn came, the QVC host turned to me and said, "Tell us about the Miracle Mop." I did what came naturally to me in talking about the product, as I had done in any number of live appearances. I started to talk right from my heart and the phones just started to light up. The QVC phone system went absolutely crazy with thousands and thousands of calls. The operators couldn't keep up with the calls. People couldn't order the Miracle Mop fast enough. We sold 18,000 mops in 20 minutes. My company had to work 24 hours a day to keep up with the demand. Since then, we've sold more than three million Miracle Mops and it became one of the top-selling products on QVC.

If you are going to run a corporation and achieve growth and long-term stability, you must have the skills not only in your area of expertise, but strong leadership and people skills as well. You must have a sixth sense when it comes to risk-taking, problem solving, and decision making.

Joy has a straightforward explanation for what happened in her February 1993 television debut: one, the product is "fabulous"; two, "People identify with me because I'm a regular person like them, with cleaning and household needs, the same as anybody else out there. I tell them that here's a quality product and that I'm going to show them what it does." Joy's vice president for product planning, Jan Wathey, who accompanies her on personal appearances, adds her firsthand report on why Joy succeeded so famously and why she continues to do so: "There's a trust factor that she generates. When she goes on the air, you see a genuine person who believes in her product and her excitement shows through. That's exactly why she sells so well. She believes so heartily in every product she produces."

The Miracle Mop and the other "original, unique and innovative products" produced by Joy's Long Island company, Ingenious Designs, are in the best of hands—their inventor, manufacturer, and marketer. Since launching her company in 1990 at the age of 33 in the back of the auto body shop attached to her father's bus company, Joy has logged $80 million in sales. It's been a meteoric climb from first-year sales of $6,000.

> *Don't let anyone tell you that you can't take one small step at a time in the beginning. I hired my first production employee from a local church with the cooperation of the pastor who put up a Help Wanted sign. The company started with very little money and some very good ideas for new products. The first couple of years were run at a loss because of investments in engineering, molds, production, setup, etc., but then sales started to turn around fast after my appearances on QVC. I worked personally in all steps of the operation—including sourcing of raw material. This was critical since my goal was to produce the best quality products at the best value for customers.*
>
> *We started off by investing under $100,000 of savings and I personally searched for and found skilled engineers and mold makers. Then with input from seasoned production and product experts, we built the best mop we could imagine. In the process, it took several years to be profitable.*

If I could re-visit my start-up years, I would change two things at the very least. First, I would analyze profitability more accurately to reflect costs that I now know come further down the road. Second, I would have timed new ventures so that each would support the next. Then I would have had a much greater ability to support the cost of moving into traditional retail in a more timely manner. When a product is moving from electronic retailing into the stores, the timing and expense to achieve that is critical.

The inventor side of Joy is traceable to the age of 10, and the big idea that got away goes back to the age of 16. One evening while she was working part-time at an animal hospital, a dog was brought in after being hit on a dark road by a car. Joy had the bright idea that a fluorescent dog collar could prevent such nighttime accidents. Realizing that animal owners might not buy such an item separately, she conceived of adding fluorescence to a flea collar. Too young and inexperienced and lacking capital, she gave up on the idea only to see it marketed one year later by a major pet supply company. Her reaction added entrepreneur to inventor: "I told myself the next time I had a good idea, I would bring it to market." As a result, what she calls a "joint personality" was born—both inventor and entrepreneur.

Inventing is something that came as natural to me as music to somebody who's musically-inclined. It just seemed a natural thing for me every time I would look at something, I would create something better or different back at home. I was always fiddling with contraptions and things like that. I also began to realize that I had a business mind. I became intrigued by management styles and the challenge of business opportunities. At Pace University, I studied business

> *administration and after college went to work for Eastern Airlines. Even as full-time mother and housewife, I became involved in organization work as president of one of the largest parent-teacher associations in the state of New York. So, when the time came, it was very easy for me to follow the road of not only designing products but also running the business of making and selling them. Many inventors will hire people to make their products. I took on the task of creating a company to make my own inventions, and everything grew from there.*

The jewel in the company crown—a mop—epitomizes her success as an inventor, her determination as an entrepreneur, and her talent for marketing. In inventing marketable products, she has followed a standard formula of building a better mousetrap based on her own experience and observation. The mop developed from her chores in boating and housekeeping. When she went boating (a favorite pastime), she was often swabbing the deck and continually wringing out the mop. The inventor kicked in: there had to be a better way. So she developed the self-wringing Marine Mop, which worked fine, but didn't generate many sales. Then the entrepreneur in Joy stepped in. She converted the mop to home use based on her experience as a housekeeping mother of three in suburban Long Island. She was cleaning the floor with mops that didn't last very long and had to be supplemented with paper towels and sponges. There had to be a better way.

> *Miracle Mop was from my day-to-day life. When I invented and designed this product, I realized that there wasn't a quality mop on the market that did what the Miracle Mop does—with its self-wringing action and all its other features. I was throwing away mop after mop every few months. I saw the need for a*

quality mop and after developing the idea for my mop, I started contacting people in the traditional retail area industry, who said that nobody's going to pay $20 for a mop, that nobody's going to pay more than a couple of dollars for a mop. I said NO—if people realize that they're getting a quality mop that is literally the last mop they'll ever have to buy, they'll pay for it because their floors are just as important as their carpets and they will pay over one hundred dollars for a vacuum.

Joy looks upon her products as "staples," items that people will buy for themselves, their home, or for spouses and children. Where there's a mop, there's bound to be a bucket. Joy's version is the Tuck'it Bucket, which is not round, but rectangular. It holds steady with any size mop handle, won't tip over, and is designed to be emptied without spilling over the sides. There's more to the bucket: It doubles as a paint bucket with a grid to clean excess paint off. It popped into Joy's mind when she became aware "that there wasn't a quality bucket that had features a bucket should have, such as holding the mop up so it doesn't spill over if you have to answer the phone when you're mopping."

I believe the human elements in business are critical in the success of a company. The spirit of an organization is a primary driving force.

Moving to another room in the house, there is the Jewel Kit: "It keeps your jewelry organized." It has 14 interlocking compartments made of durable luxurious plastic with a velvety interior that can hold more than 150 items—

rings, bracelets, and necklaces, separate and untangled, easy to locate in 200 cubic inches of storage space. Rolled up, it's under five inches high and when opened, it displays all the jewelry it's storing. The Jewel Kit's sibling is the Rolykit, a roll-up case that can have as many as 38 adjustable compartments to hold—you name it—hardware, household and automotive tools, office supplies, sporting equipment, toys, cosmetics, or jewelry. As to necklace clasps, Joy invented a clasp that can itself be worn as a piece of jewelry. It is reversible to dress up or down an outfit and is interchangeable between a strand of pearls or a herringbone chain (which are sold in Joy's Signature Series of fashion jewelry).

As with all idea people, Joy doesn't (and can't) set a boundary between idea time and *other* time. Ideas pop up anytime, anywhere. It's a mark of the entrepreneur in her. She's always in the habit of looking for a better way, a better product, a better solution. It can happen on a park bench, for example.

> *While on vacation, I was sitting on a bench in East Hampton, Long Island, in front of a very exclusive bakery shop when I saw a gentleman walk out with two pies in separate cardboard boxes. It dawned on me that the typical bakery containers hadn't changed in something like 50 years. They haven't been enhanced. There was nothing new or unusual about them and they had no repeat use. I speculated on where he was going to put the two pies if he goes to someone's house. Suppose he wants to take one of them to his own house. What will he do? I realized that what was needed was a bakery box that was able to fold for storing until you use it the next time. So I began thinking about a new bakery box. I went back to my house and started drawing design sketches. By the time the night ended, I realized I wanted a box that for the first time was able to fold flat for storing,*

since there's never enough room in anybody's kitchen. We created the Piatto Bakery Box which is not only collapsible, but is a designer bakery box with a removable shelf so it can hold two pies. It goes 10 steps further than the traditional cake box—and it's dishwasher safe!

Joy developed a box to hold homemade bakery goods that are brought along when visiting family and friends or usable for home storage. Its 11-by-6-inch hexagonal shape unfolds, opens, and snaps into place. Add the shelf and it holds two pies or two dozen cupcakes or muffins. Aptly named the Piatto ("flat" in Italian) Bakery Box, it comes in wine, gold, or hunter green, and it is backed by Joy's testimonial and company motto: "A graceful expression for those who put time and love into the foods they bake. I know it will 'Make Your Space A Better Place.'"

According to Joy, her ideas "come out inevitably wherever, whenever after a certain amount of time."

It all depends on where I am and what I'm doing. I was at dinner in a Japanese restaurant recently and before we knew it the conversation got around to talking about how the spoons we were using made so much more sense than all the spoons we have in our kitchen drawers at home. So we all started talking about making a utensil set that makes more sense than the utensils we now use. The show hosts on QVC have a standing joke when they introduce me. They say that they like me to take nice long showers because I get all my ideas in the shower. Actually, I only got an inspiration for one of my ideas in the shower. But it is true that my mind is always on my business. I don't sleep a lot and will sit on my front porch or my back deck late into the night. There is always something going on in my brain, whether it's what we have to do to get a product out the door or an idea for the right packaging or a new product or an enhancement for a product we already have.

As housewife and entrepreneur, she begins her work-day as a single parent and mother of three teenagers and then switches to chairman, president, and owner of Ingenious Designs. At company headquarters, she describes herself as a hands-on executive who follows through on everything "step by step, every step of the way."

I'm up at 5:30 in the morning as part of a household of three teenagers getting ready for school. They leave very early and I leave right behind them. I'm in the office anywhere between 7:30 and 8:30. And then I begin my day—everything that's on my plate, from reading contracts to dealing with production deadlines, from sales presentations to product or packaging design. Sales, operations, finance—I deal with the business decisions that any other corporate leader has to deal with. All before lunch. I'm also very involved in TV commercials and live appearances for our products.

I'm never able to leave my office for long, except to go to the plant or to the executive conference room next to my office. I'm never even able to eat in our company lunchroom. I never have time to go there, except to sing happy birthday to someone. I eat my lunch at my desk, anywhere between 1:00 and 4:00 in the afternoon, whenever I can manage it. My mother now makes me a salad because she feels so bad that I don't eat properly. If my daughters are cheerleading or my son is in sports, I will make it a point to leave by about 6:00 or thereabouts. But otherwise I'm usually here till 7, 8, or 9 or 10:00.

If you are going to run a corporation and achieve growth and long-term stability, you must have the skills not only in your area of expertise, but strong leadership and people skills as well. You must have a sixth sense when it comes to risk-taking, problem solving and decision making.

At the office, one of the most exciting things for me is getting into a room with all the brilliant minds that I have here and coming up with new ways to do things. We talk about all the challenges of doing business. I have ideas and concepts, but I need engineers—I've always had them—to do the formal drawings. I tell them what I want and they tell me it's impossible. We get through that and come up with the product.

Joy counts heavily on another dimension in her business success—the emotional support of family and friends on and off the job. They both support and free her, starting with her mother, father, and brother, who all work with her in the company. Her brother, John Martorella, joined the company in 1996 as executive vice president, and her parents are in administrative positions. Her father, who owned the Long Island Bus Company, provides a seasoned business voice in policy decisions. Joy doesn't "know how people can go through life as the *hard* business person who rules as opposed to guiding people." She rates emotional support as a major business asset.

It would be impossible for me to have this tremendous success and peace of mind and strength to do what I do without the support and the pride that I have from my children and the people that surround me at the company. I listen to my children talk to their friends about me and I just can't believe they're talking about me. They're so proud. They are right-on kids, straight A students, very caring and loving. They're just wonderful and wonderfully supportive. That frees up my mind, which is important since my schedule is tough and I do a lot of traveling.

> *At the company, all the faith and talent I have around me enables me to do so much more and accomplish so much more in shorter spans of time and that to me is one of the keys to my success. A majority of the people who work for me are friends that I've known for years and I've hired them for their expertise and talents. I've been fortunate enough to have very talented friends who enhance what I do. I have the most exciting and talented staff that any business leader could have. It is unbelievable. I don't know how, but the spirit of what we do just filters through this building. I am convinced that this goes a long way in dealing with people we do business with. They can sense our honest, hard-working and responsive approach in any venture together. I believe the human elements in business are critical in the success of a company. The spirit of an organization is a primary driving force.*

From the retailing perspective, Joy realizes that she's at a "unique time and place in history." The home shopping phenomenon has opened up unprecedented opportunities to reach an international audience with her inventive products. She readily acknowledges that QVC is a significant part of her company's success, reaching, as it does, into 67 million homes. Her QVC experience is a case study in how electronic retailing can tilt the scale in favor of entrepreneurs with consumer products to sell.

At QVC, Briggs points to the opportunities that a company like his provides up-and-coming entrepreneurs with its "strategy of seeking out new products and giving them a chance on TV." Small companies can play David to the Goliaths of consumer products by selling their products to QVC as they would to a department store. In buying products from a company and selling them at a markup from wholesale, QVC not only provides revenues for a company, it also puts the TV spotlight on products that would otherwise pass unnoticed in the crowded consumer marketplace. But there's no guaranteeing success. Take it from Briggs: "This is a very humbling business. Many things that you think will work don't live up to your expectations. Other things that you think are so-so turn out to be big winners. The customer votes and the product is what counts."

I came in to meet with QVC . . . and was told that they wanted to return the Miracle Mop [because] it wasn't selling [fast enough]. . . . I knew that it would sell if I demonstrated it. So I said to them, "Let me get on TV with it and I'll show you what an exciting product it is." I started to talk right from my heart and the phones just started to light up. . . . We sold 18,000 mops in 20 minutes. . . .

Joy's success demonstrates the power of QVC. She introduces her products on TV to jump-start their introduction into retail stores. Her products are particularly well suited to QVC because they require and/or benefit from demonstration. Briggs cites her "terrific knack for identifying what consumers want to buy" and her talent for demonstrating her products. Joy advises aspiring entrepreneurs who take the electronic retailing route to have "a great product at a great price and the ability to demonstrate it." Drawing on her experiences, she has identified principles of success that have worked for her and can work for others:

- Focus on the product and deliver quality. "The product is always king. If you want a long-term relationship with the consumer, you must have quality products."
- Try to achieve a measure for quality in the venue that is appropriate for a product, such as earning the *Good Housekeeping* Seal. This means a lot to Joy, and she places a high priority on earning the seal for her products.
- Emphasize the USA label. Joy promotes her products as "Proudly Made In The USA."
- Personalize the product. "We've given our products a human aspect and that makes a lot of marketing sense to me." The importance of the personal link is confirmed by the many letters Joy receives. "More than anything else in the letters I receive, I get the message, 'Joy, you're an honest business person. I think you make quality products and you stand behind them. That means a lot to me as a customer.' "

Excerpts from these letters confirm these lessons of successful marketing for all entrepreneurs:

> *Just a note to let you know what wonderful products you have created.*
>
> (from Georgia)

> *I brought my first batch of cupcakes into my office this morning [in a Piatto Bakery Box]. Everyone I work with is thrilled to see me carrying my "gold hatbox" into the office. Four people in my office now own Piattos of their own, two of them as gifts from me.*
>
> (from Long Island)

*I love all of Joy's inventions and look forward to her
new inventions.*

(from North Carolina)

In marketing her better mousetraps, Joy shows what
her products can do—on home shopping TV, in commercials, and in promotion videos at department stores. In
the early years of her company, she was continually on
the move, making live appearances and demonstrations.
Currently, because there is only so much of her time to go
around (although, like the typical entrepreneur, there's
no shortage of energy), she has cut public appearances to
a minimum to concentrate on making TV commercials;
on her live QVC appearances; and on her hour-long program, *Make Your Space A Better Place.* (She also appears
live in Europe on QVC, where her program is called *Ingenious Designs.*) Overall, the emphasis is on leveraging her
marketing talents.

> *When I took Miracle Mop to QVC, which as an elec-
> tronic retailer reaches millions of people, I was able to
> stand up in front of a huge audience on live TV and
> demonstrate Miracle Mop. My TV demonstrations
> made history and together we created the Miracle Mop
> commercial, which became one of the most successful
> direct response commercials ever. The Miracle Mop
> created a mopping craze throughout the world. All of a
> sudden you started hearing about all these new mops
> and seeing them all over TV.*

Inevitably, Joy has become known as the "Mop Lady"
wherever she goes. There is no escape. She has become a
different kind of celebrity, not a distant figure but someone her enthusiastic customers look upon as the neighbor next door. Such as the vacation in Aruba when she
and her three children were watching the television
screen in an airport lounge while waiting to board their

plane back to the United States. On came the commercial with Joy talking up a storm for her mop. Her children sank in their seats with embarrassment as all eyes turned to Joy. Here in person was the woman on TV in the airport lounge waiting room. People came over and reported that they have the Miracle Mop and raved about the product. They talked to her as someone they knew, as a personal friend. At the same time, the airport encounter became an impromptu marketing event.

> *I realize that as spokesperson for the company I'm a large part of its visibility. I am the person who appears on TV and that is where my products appear first. Then they go into retail where we now have a very strong base. We have linked up with retail Goliaths like Bloomingdale's, Bed Bath & Beyond, Home Depot and Kmart, and benefit from their sophisticated marketing techniques. We provide demonstrations in retail stores as well as videos which show how our products work.*

The producer of prize-winning commercials for Joy, Sheila James describes her as a dream demonstrator, with lessons for all entrepreneurs to learn in selling their products via television. "Joy gets the medium out of the way so that her personality comes through with an immediacy that actors can't achieve," Sheila reports, based on her years of experience. "What you want to achieve in direct selling is credibility and reality. When people say what's in their minds, rather than what's written down, it comes through from their heart, their eyes. It has immediacy. You can't find an actor who can play a spokesperson the way Joy can in her own words and style. She really believes what she's saying and people realize that someone real is speaking to them. People say, 'I believe that lady.' She is like the person in your family that you trust and listen to."

Sheila recalls what the skeptics said about putting Joy on national television. They said that she's obviously from New York and people don't trust or believe New Yorkers. Joy confounded them, Sheila reports. The effect was "unbelievably positive." The same thing happened when Joy appeared in England on QVC. Once again, she demonstrated that it counts to be what Sheila calls "real." Record-breaking sales confirmed it in England and wherever else she appeared in Europe.

. . . My mind is always on my business. I don't sleep a lot and will sit on my front porch or my back deck late into the night. There is always something going on in my brain, whether it's what we have to do to get a product out the door or an idea for the right packaging or a new product or an enhancement for a product we already have.

For entrepreneurs going on camera, Sheila offers this advice: "First, think carefully and seriously about your product and its benefits to consumers, about what it will do for them. When you go before the television camera, you want to be talking to one person, sitting there in a room looking at you. Speak to that person as you would to someone that you'll help with your product. Convey the enthusiasm they will feel when they use the product. It is one person talking to one person."

Back at the office, Joy's brother and executive vice president helps to complete a close-up of Joy as entrepreneur-inventor. She's a "bundle of energy and an unwavering optimist who sets her goals and then commits herself to reaching them." As for the company, he points to a new direction that's in keeping with the goal of turning out products that make a difference in the home. Now that Ingenious Designs has a well-established marketing style and strategy that combines home shopping television and retail sales, the company has its "eyes open to adding other company's products that have a unique twist and fit its offerings," but, thus far, have gone largely unnoticed in the marketplace.

In looking ahead, Joy builds on her three-part role as inventor, manufacturer, and marketer:

1. "To answer needs that could not be satisfied in the past by a product."
2. To keep turning out "products that offer quality, functionality, value and are proudly made in the USA."
3. "To branch out further into the retail market. We have a whole big world out there."

MARY ELLEN SHEETS— TWO MEN AND A TRUCK

"Owning a Business Is Like Owning the Greatest Toy in the World"

5

MARY ELLEN SHEETS— TWO MEN AND A TRUCK

"Owning a Business Is Like Owning the Greatest Toy in the World"

On a quiet springtime Sunday in East Lansing, Michigan, a well-groomed woman on a pink moped was on the way to deposit $7,000 in the 24-hour slot at the local bank when her bag of cash and checks flew off the back of the bike. In retrospect, the two-wheeled entrepreneur chuckles over the episode, but at the time one frantic lady was running around, chasing the receipts for her business. "They were a weekend's receipts," Mary Ellen Sheets recalls. "Once we got going no one could believe how much money we made."

In fact, her entire situation was—at least—slightly unbelievable. A woman, whose day job was data systems analyst for the State of Michigan, was running, of all things, a local moving business in an industry in which no women were visible and certainly not welcome.

In 1988, only three years after starting a business in which all she has ever invested was $350, she had five trucks on the road, with many millions in revenues on the horizon from nationwide franchising (projected to reach $100 million by the turn of the century).

Initially, hers was a mom-and-mom operation. The "headquarters" of her company, Two Men and A Truck, consisted of Mary Ellen moonlighting out of her condo apartment and her mother's back porch. That's where her movers left each day's receipts in a box made to hold firewood. Her mother, in her mid-80s, kept an eye on the comings and goings of the per diem movers, who parked their cars in her backyard before switching to one of the trucks waiting for them.

Actually, the first two "men" with a truck were teenagers—Mary Ellen's sons, one just old enough to drive, both trying to earn spending money.

> *I became, to my surprise, a single mother, all of a sudden divorced, with two sons and a daughter. The boys wanted to earn their own spending money and I tried to help them. When their father left, he left an old green pickup truck that we bought from Michigan State University. The school used it on the campus grounds. The boys wanted to use it to move people so I put a little ad in our local shopping guide and that's how it all started. The first line of the ad was Two Men and A Truck, though they weren't men. Brig, the older, was just 16 and Jon was 13. I also made a form for the boys so they could keep track of things—people's address, what they wanted moved. I sat down at the kitchen table and drew a logo on top of the moving sheet. It's still our logo, a stick figure black-and-white drawing of the front of a truck with two people sitting in front. It was a silly moving sheet. Among the list of items to move, I included an elephant.*
>
> *The boys charged $25 an hour and every time they moved someone they had to put three dollars in a little dish in the kitchen to buy gas. They split the rest, which was pretty good spending money for kids. Just being kids, if they told someone they would move them, but wanted to go to a party instead, they'd just*

call the people and say that someone stole the truck or it broke down. That's the kind of outfit it was. When Brig went off to North Michigan University, his younger brother, Jon, did some moving with his friends, but then he, too, went off to college. After they were both gone, the phone calls still kept coming in. It's amazing how the name caught on and people took it to heart.

As to aspiring entrepreneurs, my advice is to just keep plugging away! . . . You can't open a lemonade stand and just sit there waiting for someone to come. You have to run out in the road and flag people down!

I decided to buy a used truck, very used, and continue the moving. It was in May 1985 and the truck cost $350. That was my first and only investment in the business. I bought the truck from the owner of a furniture store. The gas gauge didn't work so every night I had to make sure to fill the tank. I advertised for manpower in the local paper and hired two men at $10 an hour. I let them know each day whether they had a moving job and paid them in cash every night. They were not the quality of people we have now, just two people who wanted jobs. We learned as we went along and slowly developed our own way of what we found was the best way to do things.

As a business success, Mary Ellen Sheets stands out as a paradox based on improvisation, but also as a model of grassroots, do-it-yourself entrepreneurship built on personality, energy, and skill. As to helping her sons earn pocket money, it came naturally.

> *When I was a little kid, my mother would have me go door to door selling eggs and tomatoes out of a wagon. We lived by the golf course and I'd pick up balls and sell them. I also remember answering the phone for my father. He owned a bus line, a fleet of local buses. People used to call and ask about the schedule. We were all trained to answer the phone and recite the bus schedule.*

As to the moving business, she was an accidental entrepreneur who practiced just-in-time learning, staying one step ahead of the consequences of any missteps that were the result of not knowing the rules and regulations. You can say her moving business just happened, but you can't say she was not equipped for business. Her work as a systems analyst prepared her to design an efficient and well-organized moving system. Her stint as an office manager developed administrative skills. She knows how to analyze numbers and deal with data. Her volunteering to handle the phones in a hospital crisis intervention center honed skills in dealing with people on the phone. In developing Two Men and A Truck, she emerged as a smart, savvy, hard-driving entrepreneur who identified opportunity and went where it took her— from local mover to national franchiser.

In one sense, her success was cumulative, not really haphazard. Built on unbridled ambition? Not at all. Bottom line–focused? Only as necessary. At the end of her first year in business, she chalked up $1,000 in profits and gave it all away in 10 charity donations so she wouldn't have to deal with taxes. Committed? Unquestionably—and she remembers distinctly the upsetting night she became aware of her commitment.

Several years ago, while we were limited to local moving, a man phoned after we had damaged his furniture. He just got madder and madder. I tried to calm him down, using skills I had learned as a counselor who listened to people on the phone. When someone's really upset, let them unload and they will calm down. But it didn't work with him. He just got madder. Finally, he said that he was on the board of the bank and that he was going to call the local newspaper and tell them what a terrible company we were.

It was quite late at night and it left me so shaken that I called my brother. I told him, "I'm just so upset. This guy's gonna ruin my business," and my brother said, "Mary Ellen, sell that stupid business. You've got a good job, work at it." I got so mad at my brother. It was like, Are you crazy? I'm not selling this business. I realized then that I really loved the business. I think that's the only time I got really discouraged. But most of the time, things are great. People are happy and they love our service. We've gotten a lot of "Ata boys!" and a lot of nice feedback. Once the business got started, I tweaked it here and there and saw it improve. I just tried to do something every day to make it a little better. I just loved it. It was so much fun. Owning a business is like owning the greatest toy in the world.

As a glimpse into the life, times, and struggles of a fledgling entrepreneur, excerpts from Mary Ellen's diaries in the months after the May 1985 launch of her business describe her ups and downs and the persistence that characterizes the entrepreneur:

Mild exultation—*9/28/85—Two moving trucks out!*
Problem and profit in the making—*9/30/85—One truck has to have head gasket. I took in $3,400 this month!*

More problems—*10/1/85—Truck still broken down. Irate customers. 10/3/85—Customer told me to kiss my butt! Had truck hauled to Mt. Hope garage.*

Pressure—*10/16/85, 9 p.m.—Had to find movers for tomorrow. This is hard work, but I think it's worth it. Never have a minute for myself.*

Slowdown—*10/20/85—Moving business letting up.*

Problem again—*10/22/85—Was going to an auction, but never got to go because mover's truck wouldn't start. Finally had it hauled to Mt. Hope garage. Some days are like that!*

Expansion?—*10/25/85—Wrote "specs" for movers. Me—buy new truck???*

All in a day's work—*10/31/85—Truck troubles. Advertising went from $7.00 a week to $12.81! Guys at hardware store gave me an expensive dolly ($230) in exchange for short one ($162). Letter from irate customer.*

Downer—*11/1/85—Customer Check bounced. Having a business makes me weepy.*

The next year, 1986, was a time of familiar entrepreneurial growing pains: laws, rules, regulations, red tape, and competition:

9/7/86—Police called. They arrested Joe [one of her movers] for not having a driver's license. Had to go to police station and get truck keys. Reading security commission rules for moving business. Egad, it's almost impossible!!! What will I do?

11/22/86—Customer told me that City Wide Movers is advertising as "Two Men and a Truck"! GRRR. Can they do that?

11/24/86—City Wide Movers are copying my ads in the Shoppers' Guide. Enlarge all my ads.

> *12/2/86—Got workmen's compensation for Joe—*
> *one of my biggest worries. Bruce [attorney friend] is*
> *going to write to City Wide Movers. Saving my ass!*

Then, in 1987, moments of truth—grow or decline.
Decisions, decisions, decisions.

> *1/3/87—Computer screwed up at night, but I got it*
> *to go!*
> *1/16/87—Bought 18-foot truck at Bud Kouts. Had*
> *long interesting talk with finance manager.*
> *7/12/87—Cost $1,000 to replace a damaged table*
> *for customer.*
> *10/3/87—Met with John Dodge, owner of Sneak-*
> *ers, about franchising. [Dodge taught franchising at*
> *local community college.] I learned:*
> *it costs a lot;*
> *time-consuming;*
> *I'm not ready.*
> *Worked on books. Playing with my payroll program.*
> *12/5/87—Met with Ray Damas [attorney] from*
> *3:30 to 7:30 about franchising. How exciting.*
> *$30,000, but sounds good. I have to select a new*
> *name. Talked to Jon for a long time. He's excited*
> *about franchise.*
> *12/31/87—My mind is in turmoil about quitting my*
> *job. I want to so bad, but I'm so scared.*

By instinct more than design, Mary Ellen was developing a niche in the moving industry with a distinctive formula that would make her the country's only franchiser
of local movers and owner of the fourth-largest U.S. residential moving company. She had stumbled onto a major
market, which is largely ignored by big moving companies. About 40 million individuals or families move in the
United States each year and almost half of the moves are

strictly local. The fixed overhead of large companies makes the local moving market difficult and expensive for them. They have big expensive trucks and storage facilities to maintain and ICC licenses and state permits to deal with. They also have the substantial costs of sales forces and national advertising.

On the marketing angle alone, Mary Ellen Sheets soon discovered a selling edge—the sight of her trucks. People started to call in from their car phones, intrigued by the name on the side of a truck they were following. Early on, Mary Ellen recognized her trucks as "a moving billboard that creates strong name awareness." She was establishing a branding with built-in local appeal. Her simple black logo and her company name on a white background carried the implicit message: *We're a low-overhead, hometown, family-style operation. We're not big, busy, and expensive.*

I became . . . all of a sudden divorced, with two sons and a daughter. The boys wanted to earn their own spending money and I tried to help them. . . . Their father [had] left . . . an old green pickup truck. . . . The boys wanted to use it to move people so I put a little ad in our local shopping guide and that's how it all started.

The image worked and it was true. Mary Ellen's billing formula was customer friendly. Instead of charging by weight (as was standard), she charged by the hour, which made her price highly competitive. As for damage, Two Men and A Truck did not reimburse the customer at the paltry industry standard of \$.60 per pound for damage; it made sure the damage was fixed to the customer's satisfaction. As for expensive art or antiques, she made a point of checking with customers and advising them to get a rider to cover moving risks.

As the business got going, Mary Ellen made sure her movers didn't share the stereotyped reputation of local movers as muscle men wearing dirty undershirts and sporting tattoos of dancing girls in grass skirts. She cleaned up the image of her moving men. They arrive on time, introduce themselves, looking neat and clean and behaving in a friendly, polite manner. Her trucks are impeccable and, after the first bumpy years, in good running condition. Mary Ellen developed a double-barreled formula: providing professional service while maintaining small-town friendliness and running a cash-and-carry, debt-free company.

> *After my first year, I decided to buy a new truck. When I went to the local Chevy dealer, I was so nervous. I didn't know if he would sell a woman a truck. But they were very nice and did sell me a truck. When I went to pick it, it wouldn't run! I went to another Chevy dealer and bought my truck there. Then I bought a new truck every year. Every time I did, my business would increase. It was another moving billboard on the street complete with name and phone number.*

After Mary Ellen was in business for two years, her movers would sometimes go beyond city limits to move customers north to Travers City, even to Detroit or Ohio. This brought her face-to-face with the complexities of governmental regulation and led to a characteristic Mary Ellen Sheets solution. State police stopped one of her trucks for not having a license for out-of-town moving, defined as going seven miles out of any municipality.

During her lunch hours, Mary Ellen, who was still working downtown, visited four different attorneys who specialized in transportation law: "I asked them if they could explain the law to me and they all gave me different answers. It was just crazy, and they probably thought I was crazy. So what I did was take a soup can and use it to draw a circle on a city map of Lansing. I told my drivers not to go outside the circle."

By the time she switched in 1989 from running a local moving company in Lansing to franchising, the Two Men and A Truck formula was refined and ready to roll out all over the country in one town or city after another. Still, she hesitated over franchising until she participated in a business panel.

> *Someone at Michigan State University asked me if I would join a panel discussion about business. There was another lady there who, when she heard about my moving business, told me I should franchise it. I told her that I didn't know how I could since all I had was the truck and the moving men. She had a pet feeding service and she said, "Well, all I do is feed dogs, so for God's sake if I can franchise you can, too." So she gave me the name of her attorney. I went to see him and told him all about my business and he said he would help me franchise it. I didn't even know what franchising was. He charged me something like $27,000 which I paid over time out of the money from my Lansing moving operation.*
>
> *By this time, in 1989, I was really starting a business. I had a bookkeeper. I was paying taxes and I finally got insurance on my moving men, in addition to the insurance on the trucks. Various friends had urged me to get incorporated so I wouldn't be personally liable, which I got around to doing. So as I went along, I learned to start a business and that has made it easier for me to teach other people when I got around to*

franchising. I read all those stories about people investing $200,000 and $300,000 to get a franchising company started. We never had that kind of money.

After [my sons] were both gone . . . I decided to buy a used truck . . . and continue the moving [business]. . . . The truck cost $350. That was my first and only investment in the business.

As everyone knows, moving and trucking are mostly men's business, but I didn't let it make any difference to me. I went my own way and re-invented the wheel. We did our own thing and we benefitted from word of mouth, which is how most of our franchises were sold.

In converting her business from local mover to national franchiser, Mary Ellen kept overhead to a minimum, operating out of her apartment and handling the administrative details herself. She finally quit her job to plunge into franchising.

My office was in my home. I would sleep for a few hours and then go right into the room which was my office. For the first years of franchising, I didn't know if it was day or night. I just worked like crazy. People I used to work with would call and say, "Let's go to lunch," and I'd say, "Are you crazy? I don't have time for lunch." That's what it was like and I loved it.

I was writing a company newsletter, running an annual meeting, working with my attorney who was handling the selling of franchises for me and visiting the new franchises. I had an 800 number that fran-

chisees could call any time if they had problems. I was stocking items for them to buy if they wanted. That has since become our Two Men and A Truck Pro Shop, which now stocks 60 items—company shirts, boxes, mugs, doormats—and grosses $750,000 a year. I was doing all that myself. Late in '93, I moved from my apartment to an office in an old house and hired a lady part-time to help me with filing. That stayed as company headquarters until this year (1998) when we moved into a new building that we put up. It cost nearly $600,000.

Once the business got started, I tweaked it here and there and saw it improve. I just tried to do something every day to make it a little better. . . .

To get help in running the company, Mary Ellen didn't have to look far. Her daughter, Melanie, who was a well-paid pharmaceutical rep, quit her job to join her mother in 1994. She had a strong track record in marketing and already knew the moving business as moonlighting owner of a company franchise in Detroit. In 1994, Melanie became company president, an ideal match for CEO Mary Ellen. Mind-the-store daughter works with creative, idea-generating mother—the two traits that build in longevity for start-up companies. She describes her mother as the quintessential "free spirit who enjoys life and does what she wants to do." But also someone who "knows how to make tough decisions."

Melanie represents a turning point in the company's growth. She sees herself as "whipping things in shape" as the number of franchises increase. Together, the complementary mother-daughter leadership combines the free-wheeling, ad hoc founder of the company and her well-organized, efficient daughter. Although Mary Ellen owns the company, business decisions are a family affair, involving mother, daughter, and the original movers, sons Brig and Jon—the four of them constituting the company's board of directors. Brig works full-time at headquarters as a franchise recruiter for the company, while Jon has a franchise in Grand Rapids and also runs his mother's Lansing franchise.

The four of them meet every week to discuss the business. "We all know what the issues are and we discuss them from every possible angle, especially since we all think very differently," Melanie says. "When we make decisions, they emerge as consensus decisions." The decisions have moved the franchising toward stricter controls and toward policies that are uniform throughout the company and maintain quality service. The consensus approach and the checks and balances of the four family members has carried Two Men and A Truck past the pitfalls of many entrepreneurial companies that achieve early momentum and falter in the later stages of stabilizing their operations.

The company has made an impact in the moving industry by professionalizing local moving and raising the level of local moving men. Overall, the cross section of franchisees ranges from early retirees who want to stay active to recent college graduates who want to own a business rather than work for a big one. The young franchise owners are among the most successful. Melanie describes them as "open-minded, energetic" and as having "fire in their belly." Two Men and A Truck has also brought women into the industry; half of its franchises are owned by women or husband-and-wife partnerships.

Based on her experiences and observations, Mary Ellen has learned a lesson or two about women in business and also has advice for aspiring entrepreneurs:

One thing I know about women in business. They don't charge enough. They undercut themselves. They do a good job and should make sure they get what they deserve. Also, when you start in business, you have to be careful not to listen to negative comments. There were a lot of people who made fun of me because I had a moving business. When I franchised, they really hooted over that. I guess they don't laugh now.

When [an acquaintance] heard about my moving business, [she] told me I should franchise it. I told her that I didn't know how I could since all I had was the truck and the moving men. . . . She said, "Well, all I do is feed dogs, so for God's sake if I can franchise you can, too."

I'd tell anyone going into business: do something you like and do a little bit every day to make it better. When I was building the business, I always tried to do something. If I didn't have the money to put an ad in the paper, maybe I'd catch up on filing, clean out a drawer, call someone. You will end up doing an awful lot that way and you will realize it when you look back.

As to aspiring entrepreneurs, my advice is to just keep plugging away! I was so excited about my business that it was no effort for me to do so. Every little crack I saw, I hurried to fix. I jumped on every opportunity. I was always thinking of things to make us better. You can't open a lemonade stand and just sit there waiting for someone to come. You have to run out in the road and flag people down!

Two Men and A Truck, which targets cities of 300,000 to 500,000 as its ideal market size, makes a strong case for franchising. The company cites, for example, a Gallup Poll that reported that a franchise start-up had a 94 percent chance of succeeding versus a 10 percent chance for a nonfranchise start-up after five years of operation. The success of its own franchisees strengthens the company's case. In 1997, several of them grossed more than $1 million in revenues in a business in which the net profit ranges from 10 to 20 percent (not taking into account salaries that operating owners pay themselves). To sign up, franchisees pay an initial fee of $25,000 for exclusive rights in their local market as part of total start-up costs of $70,600 to $188,600, which include two or more trucks and all their equipment. Once in business, they pay Two Men and A Truck a 6 percent royalty on gross monthly income and a 1 percent advertising fee.

When you start in business, you have to be careful not to listen to negative comments. There were a lot of people who made fun of me because I had a moving business. When I franchised, they really hooted over that. I guess they don't laugh now.

In signing up, franchisees fill out a confidential application that taps both personal and business information, ranging from training and education to work experience, from *why* they want to invest to *how* they're going to be involved in the business. Personality questions ask about strengths and weaknesses and what applicants liked or disliked about past jobs or businesses. Credit, business, and personal references are required as well as complete financial information.

Applicants are also asked to hold up a mirror to themselves and rate themselves on a scale of 1 to 5. It's a full inventory of traits and skills: independent, motivated, management, technical, creative, problem solver, self-confident, energetic, money-oriented, decision maker, people-oriented, communicator, determined, patient, crisis manager, achiever, detailed, sales/marketing, intellectual, leader.

Each franchisee is an individualized version of an entrepreneur bound together by a common desire to have a business of his or her own. Each provides an insight into the entrepreneurial personality. A former executive for McDonald's Restaurants gravitated to the moving business "because it offers something new and different every day." An executive at a Fortune 500 Company for 16 years "was looking for something that would let me use my employee management and customer relations skills." For him: "Moving was the perfect match and Two Men and A Truck was the best company to partner with because of the excellent name and strong support systems. The best part is the freedom of owning your own business and having systems in place to run the company." A nurse and her husband who together operated a family farm wanted to earn more money by building their own business. They like the fact that they're "able to build something for themselves." A newspaper graphic artist wanting to start a business chose franchising as "the smartest route to start a new company because you avoid many of the problems of getting a new business going." Adds Mary Ellen: "Three of our franchisees are CPA's. We must be doing something right!"

Once franchisees sign on, they attend a five-day training session, which covers the full spectrum of what they need to know and do to make a success of the business. What Mary Ellen learned by doing is now presented in an intensive series of sessions that are a long way from the taken-for-granted operation that collected its receipts at a back porch in Lansing.

Monday—operations manual, forms, box ordering, signage, management, employee handbooks, and employee forms.

Tuesday—marketing and advertising, interviewing and hiring, performance reviews, and motivation.

Wednesday—communication and listening skills, scheduling and forms, difficult moves, handling upset customers, boxes, and packing.

Thursday—estimates, employee training/spot checks, and equipment/truck checkout.

Friday—marketing and advertising, safety and safety equipment, and field consultant visits.

The training takes place at the company's "Stick Men University," a 3,200-square-foot layout that handles up to 50 "students," who attend sessions and can practice handling pianos and particleboard furniture around tight spots and up stairways. They can also work with a training truck to brush up on the latest packing techniques and safety measures. Franchise owners and employees—new and old—come and learn in line with Mary Ellen's mutually serving goal for her company: "When the franchisees succeed, we succeed. It's that simple." In practical terms, that means getting behind franchise owners, building a bond with them, and maintaining quality control:

We're a friendly company, family operated and our franchisees are a part of our family. It's important that they do well. We don't deal in a lot of hype and hoopla. It's not our style. We have a formula for conducting business that has proven itself. We have the best and most comprehensive training program, supporting every part of the operation. We provide onsite visits by experienced field consultants, annual meetings where franchisees exchange business ideas, training programs throughout the year, one-on-one assistance with marketing and advertising and an 800 Help Line.

One thing we've done from the start of franchising is track all our moving jobs. Every person we move—and we moved 82,000 customers in 1997—gets a reply card and it comes here to the home office. So we know where they heard about us and how they feel about our moving service. I used to read every one of those cards. Now we have a big scanner that reads them. We still track everything in the business. Our trucks have signs on the back asking, HOW'S MY DRIVING? We have sales consultants at headquarters who visit all our franchises twice a year. If there's a problem, it comes right to the home office. Thank God there aren't very many, but if there are any we notify franchise owners immediately so they can do something about them.

Mary Ellen, who still works 40 to 50 hours a week, not only minds the business; she also shapes the mood of the headquarters operation. Sally Degnan, as the company's first employee, doesn't see any change in Mary Ellen as an upward-bound entrepreneur who leads and motivates. She's the same "kind, generous, and warm-hearted person, someone who would never ask you to do something she wouldn't do." Sally describes headquarters as a place filled with "a lot of hard work and a lot of laughter." Mary Ellen insists on seeing the humor in what's happening, which qualifies as a useful trait in a business where so many things can go wrong—from a flat tire to a chipped vase. Sally has heard Mary Ellen say time and again at company headquarters: "If we go a day without laughing in this building, we will turn off the lights, close the doors and shut down the place. If we're not going to have fun at this, then we might as well not do it."

Behind the fun, there is the drive to build the business, with innovation as well as more franchises, such as a Box Outlet with everything that do-it-yourself packers need. Or a packing service for people who don't want to do it themselves. Or a complete moving service as described by Mary Ellen: "How would you like us to come in, pack your belongings, move them to your new home and unpack them? You could come home from work in the evening to your new home and your dishes would be put away, beds made and pictures hung on the wall."

The company envisions hundreds of attractive opportunities for additional franchises, all locally based. With 70 at the end of 1998 and projected earnings of $40 million, Two Men and A Truck expects to add franchises at the rate of 15 to 20 a year. Looking ahead to the year 2000, that works out to at least 100 franchises with annual company revenues of $80 million. With an immediate eye on Canada, the corporate name has been changed from Two Men and A Truck/USA to Two Men and A Truck/ International. CEO Mary Ellen minces no words in setting her sights: "Expand. Expand. Expand."

DORIS CHRISTOPHER—
THE PAMPERED CHEF, LTD.

"The Kitchen Store
That Comes to Your Door"

6

DORIS CHRISTOPHER—
THE PAMPERED CHEF, LTD.

"The Kitchen Store
That Comes to Your Door"

On a rainy October afternoon, a suburban housewife in River Forest, Illinois, was driving her Plymouth Volare loaded down with kitchenware to a friend's home in nearby Elmhurst. She was alone, there being no room for anyone else in a car crammed with six crates of products she planned to demonstrate and—hope against hope—sell at a friend's home. A troubled expression on Doris Christopher's face reflected the *What am I doing?* conversation she was having with herself. She had selling jitters.

> *I was filled with uncertainty. I remember thinking as I was driving along that this was the most unlikely situation I'd ever gotten myself into. All the way out to my friend Ruth's house, I still remember what I was thinking, "How could I ever have thought this would work. What a harebrained scheme this is. I will never do this again." But I had to go ahead because Ruth had people coming to her house and she'd invited them at my request. I couldn't go back home. I had to show up.*

Doris didn't feel any better when she reached her friend's home and started to unload her wares in the rain. As was typical then (1980), the family room where she was going to present her demonstration was in the basement, and it turned out that the stairs were too narrow for her crates. So, she had to maneuver down the steps sideways and then proceed to unload the crates, too tense to even look at the assembled women. She concentrated on arranging the items in as attractive a way as possible before turning to face the group.

> There were about 15 people sitting there and Ruth introduced me. I thought to myself, "Well, the sooner I get started, the sooner it will be over and I won't have to do this again." So I started talking. What happened was exciting to me as a former home economics teacher. The group was listening with rapt attention. One of the things I enjoyed about teaching was getting people's attention and here they weren't whispering to each other and I didn't have to say, "Sit up in the back row." They were listening, really listening. The next thing was they asked to pass things around. I thought, "My gosh! They're even helping!"
>
> I was telling them about the products I brought along and demonstrating them. In those days, frozen pizza had become a standard item so I used a pizza to demonstrate baking stones, which truthfully were one of the most amazing things I've ever used in the kitchen. You put any food on these stones and you get superior results. I did a frozen pizza on a baking stone and added some fresh veggies—which was unusual in those days. I used some of the tools I brought to cut them up. Then I prepared a vegetable tray with some fancy little garnishes and a dip in the center. As I looked around the room, I realized that I had their full attention. Then people asked me to pass around the kitchen tools so they could get a close look at them. By

the end of the evening, they had purchased nearly $175 worth of kitchenware. I never expected to sell that much. I was thrilled. But the most important thing that happened is that four of the women asked me to present demonstrations in their homes.

Three hours later—back in the Volare—Doris Christopher was talking to herself again, this time in a totally different mood. Though she might not have said so at the time, an entrepreneur was born.

The drive back home was very different from the drive out there. I was on Cloud Nine. Two of the four people who offered to arrange demonstrations were complete strangers. They had never laid eyes on me. They happened to be neighbors of Ruth. What a vote of confidence! I can honestly say business just grew from that point forward. The women at the demonstration had wonderful kitchens, but they didn't have a place to go for advice about the stuff in their kitchen drawers and they didn't have any sense about where to get the right working tools for their kitchens. They were hungry for tools that would make it easy to do what they were doing every day.

The reluctant outing and its minisuccess have mushroomed into more than 15,000 in-home demonstrations every week by Doris Christopher's sales force of 42,000 kitchen consultants (as they are called) in all 50 states. They present and produce kitchen shows, which are generating kitchenware sales that are approaching $500 million for what is now nationally known as The Pampered Chef, Ltd. The company's motto speaks for itself: "The Kitchen Store That Comes to Your Door." The kitchen consultants offer 130 products, 90 of them exclusive to The Pampered Chef, all of them selected for high quality with an eye on multipurpose. One customer favorite: a barbecue tool that flips burgers, pierces sausages, slices meat, opens bottles, and checks meats to see if they're cooked.

One of the key elements in success is having a passion for what you do. My love of my work fuels the resilience to overcome obstacles, supports my dedication to remain true to my original vision and maintains my determination to succeed.

A classic example of a made-in-the-U.S. entrepreneurial triumph with all the trimmings, The Pampered Chef is rooted not in technology, but in tradition. It started out when one mother (Doris Christopher) confronted the familiar women's dilemma of career versus family, with a determination to give family top priority. Determined to remain a stay-at-home mother, she was sending her two little daughters off to school, which freed her to look for some way to use her professional training—in her case as a home economist. She was not sure *how.* She went through a process shared by all entrepreneurs in one way or another in searching for a business enterprise, with the added requirement of wanting to stick close to home, husband, and children. The possibility of opening a store didn't appeal to her as she considered what it took: finding the right location, furnishing it, stocking it, hiring staff and, after all that investment of time and effort, you "have to sit there and wait for customers to come to you." Not for her.

The business I chose really did start as a very, very small fledgling concept, which I intended to pursue part-time. My goal was a business that would not interfere with my family priorities, something that would require about 20 hours a week. I remember thinking about it in the months before my second daughter, Kelley, would go into kindergarten. Julie, our older daughter, was already in the third grade.

I didn't want to do something that I couldn't do well. I thought about catering because I love to cook. Given that caterers provide their services on weekends and holidays, that would not fit in with my priority of being at home with my family. I tried to think about other things that would combine my particular abilities and knowledge with the family lifestyle I wanted and came up with the idea of cooking demonstrations with an inherently interesting message to deliver.

I remembered how often I was amazed when I volunteered to help friends at their get-togethers only to find that they lacked appropriate kitchen tools. My idea was to demonstrate tools with food so that people could try them out to see if they would work for them before they did any buying. Basically, it was a show-and-tell idea. When I started thinking over the idea of in-house parties, my husband, Jay, was very helpful in dialoguing with me on how to make our kitchen shows unique and exciting. He helped me realize that I could do things in whatever way I thought was best in terms of my goal—to satisfy the hunger for information.

At a Pampered Chef kitchen show, our consultants pair real food with the tools that prepare it, giving the customer an on-site demonstration of how a product works. Our customers also benefit from a "try-before-you-buy" experience. The recipes are prepared by the kitchen consultant at the show. Guests also learn meal preparation/cooking ideas, tips and techniques during the demonstration, regardless of whether or not they make a purchase. Each of our products *comes with specific use and care information, along with recipes developed by our test kitchen. This helps ensure the customer's satisfaction with the product.*

The business I chose really did start as a very, very small fledgling concept, which I intended to pursue part-time. My goal was a business that would not interfere with my family priorities, something that would require about 20 hours a week. . . . I was amazed when I volunteered to help friends at their get-togethers only to find that they lacked appropriate kitchen tools. My idea was to demonstrate the tools with food so that people could try them out to see if they would work for them before they did any buying. . . . It was a show-and-tell idea.

The other thing about our kitchen shows is that they don't involve a major commitment, as it would be the case if people sign up for a cooking class. All they have to do is say yes to an evening of refreshments and conversation with friends. One evening, not a series of lessons. And they come away feeling very satisfied with what they saw and learned. From the very beginning, a line we used on the kitchen show invitation says, "If you love to cook or hate to cook, we have something for you." It intrigued people whether they love or hate to cook. The reality is that they do cook.

I was taking simple ideas. That's always been our focus. We have never aimed at haute cuisine. *We like things very basic. They have to be simple and fast and produce dramatic results. When people see that they can produce the same results and accomplish it with the tools we offer, that becomes a winning combination.*

The interesting thing about the business was that it was so successful and so exciting from the very beginning that I had to struggle to keep it in its place. The investment of my time in the business paid off in emotional rewards immediately. But we were not a financial success overnight because the business had no cash. I started off with $3,000 borrowed on a life insurance policy and the business has never had another cash infusion. In the beginning, I identified 25 or 30 products that I could not live without in my kitchen and looked for the exact same product or a comparable (or better quality) product that I could demonstrate and sell. Naturally, as I looked around I found other products that were intriguing and useful. They became incorporated into the line.

When Doris went shopping for an inventory, she headed for Chicago's Merchandise Mart, which at the time was a major hub of wholesale showrooms for all types of products. For her, it was a "needle-in-a-haystack" experience over the course of six trips from her suburban home as she went through myriad showrooms in search of the right kitchen tools, always mindful that her total budget was only $3,000, including what it cost to print calling cards and stationery. Whenever she found what she wanted, she was concerned that the wholesaler would not take her seriously and dismiss her as a suburban housewife trying to buy wholesale for her own kitchen. But she persevered, helped by briefings from a friend who worked in the Mart and introduced her to the basics of wholesale buying: *minimum quantity, lowest opening order* (usually $100 at that time). She had to order by the dozen and pay cash, because she had no line of credit.

> *I was surprised every time they took an order because I thought they'd think I was just someone wanting the stuff at half price. But the one thing that was clear in every transaction was that as long as I paid cash up front they were ready to sell. I was so eager and naive that if they asked about what I was doing, I laid it all out. I was happy to have them listen. These whole-salers and distributors who were accustomed to deal-ing with large orders with much bigger numbers found what I wanted to do quite amusing. Very quickly, though, after about three orders, they were willing to extend a very small amount of credit. One salesman for a supplier I was using once called on me at home. Years later, he recalled to me his initial reaction: "I kept asking myself, 'Why am I wasting my time here?' "*
>
> *What really catapulted me into action was that as I started building inventory, I had to go out and sell some of it in order to have any money to buy more. What I did was re-order as I made sales. Jay and I would spend Sunday nights in the basement, check-ing the inventory and often we'd re-order on a weekly basis. In the first months, I demonstrated, sold and delivered. We had to bag all the orders and the entire family would make all the deliveries on Saturday. Jay would take off in one direction with his car and I would take off in the other with my car. I was happy doing it, but it became a bit much. Jay said to me, "We really have to ship UPS." I remember thinking that we could no longer use the wonderful little bags we were using to pack things. They were charming and every-one loved them. But we had to make the decision to ship UPS. Obviously our little delivery system was*

both taxing and inefficient. That decision was a major turning point and put us on the road where we are now—shipping millions of kitchen products.

In the spring after her October debut, Doris really went into business, though still on a very modest basis. She always knew that a one-woman enterprise can only go so far, that she needed the multiplier effect of other people demonstrating and selling, but was just as happy the way things were going. It took a May 1981 encounter with an enthusiastic listener to move awareness toward action. The woman asked a simple but challenging question, "Would you like somebody else to do this with you? I think I might be interested."

I told her that I'd have to think about it. I knew that eventually it would be wonderful to have other people join me in the business and that was what I needed. But I didn't know whether I had enough margin in the business to pay her and I didn't know how the inventory was going to work. When I was the only one doing the Kitchen Shows, I'd check the inventory on my shelf and only take along items for demonstration that I could supply. I knew I would have to work on how I handled inventory when other people were involved in the demonstrations and sales. When I got home, after I thought it through there was no doubt in my mind. The next day I phoned her and said, "Let's talk and figure things out." She was the first kitchen consultant to join me in the business. By the end of 1981, I had twelve, all of them recruited at demonstrations.

Doris was on her way. She established a commission arrangement that was based on two things: what she learned about other companies' practices and what she thought was fair for the work done. It was a process of trial and error. In the first year, she fine-tuned the commission rate two or three times. About five years into the business, she established the commission arrangement that remains the same today. It varies according to sales and, subsequently, according to the number of consultants someone recruits. When people start with the company, they earn a 20 percent commission on sales. The rate goes to 22 percent after passing $15,000 in career sales and goes higher as an individual rises in management ranks.

At first, Doris held monthly sales meetings in her home where she provided training in how to make effective presentations, demonstrated recipes, talked about the products the company was selling, and introduced new ones. Everyone joined in by exchanging experiences, asking questions, and sharing information. She even launched the company's first sales contest for the top performer. A microwave oven was the prize. She was operating out of common sense and instinct and, then, like many another entrepreneur who expanded, she turned to a trade association to find out how the pros did things.

> *I could see that the group was motivated by recognition of their achievements. I was operating out of sheer instinct. I didn't know much about direct selling and, in fact, wouldn't even have called it direct selling. We called what we did kitchen shows, although technically they are home parties. At that time, I really wasn't following closely what other companies did. Later, in 1986, I joined the Direct Selling Association (DSA), which is the nation's premier direct selling trade association. At that point, I started getting lessons at the hands of the masters. It gave me ideas on which to reflect so I could determine how we could tailor programs that would work for us and our particular company culture. I certainly have learned a lot*

from DSA and have used what I've learned as standards for what we do.

Meanwhile, back in the basement of the Christopher home, wife and husband were staying on top of what—in retrospect—was a just-in-time inventory with a homemade system. A handwritten list itemized such kitchen tools as cake tester (144 in stock); 10-inch whisk, French scraper, oil slick, and spreader (72 of each); spatter shield (48); thermometer, tea infuser, gravy strainer (12 of each). The company's inventory, which once piled up in the Christophers' basement, now fills over 660,000 square feet of warehouse space. Outgoing products require 9 UPS trucks on an average day (18 on peak days) as more than 3,000 orders a day (8,000 on peak days) are sent to customers. More than 100 "pickers" fill boxes with individual orders taken by the company's kitchen consultants.

The interesting thing about the business was that it was so successful and so exciting from the very beginning that I had to struggle to keep it in its place. The investment of my time in the business paid off in emotional rewards immediately. But we were not a financial success overnight. . . .

As the company developed, a number of factors powered its success, starting with Doris Christopher's expertise and experience. After earning a home economics degree from the University of Illinois at Urbana/Champaign, she taught high school home economics and then worked for the University of Illinois Cooperative Extension Service. As a home economist, she knows what a kitchen needs. As a good cook herself, she knows what it takes to make a good meal.

When back-to-career time came, Doris identified her imperatives as a combination of ambition and responsibilities—both family and social. Down the road, this shaped company culture and also served the company's business goals. As an entrepreneur, she needed to offer quality products that appeal to women like her and her friends. Someone in it just for the money would be tempted to cut corners, but that would violate Doris's self-image and her professional commitment. Without ambition, she wouldn't have worked so hard, once the business got rolling.

> *Since I wanted to help provide what we wanted for our family, the ambition part was very clear, but I didn't want to do something just to bring in some income. I wanted to do something that I felt good about. I wanted to use my talents to do something with a purpose. I was not interested in biding my time in a job. So both ambition and a sense of responsibility were there. One of the key elements in success is having a passion for what you do. My love of my work fuels the resilience to overcome obstacles, supports my dedication to remain true to my original vision and maintains my determination to succeed.*
>
> *I began the Pampered Chef as a flexible job opportunity that balanced my love of cooking with a strong will to keep my family as a top priority. In the beginning, I was able to set my own hours and remain completely in control of how much time I spent on the business each day. As the business began to grow beyond my expectations, I struggled with the multi-*

tude of demands placed on my time. I believe this is true of everyone who juggles a variety of priorities.

I work with a lot of women and the thing I see in women is a real sense of nurturing. I know that's what I've done with this business. I've nurtured it. I'm very emotionally attached to this business in a way I don't think many men would be attached to a business. In the beginning, I was a pretty unsophisticated business person. I didn't use business jargon. I didn't know the latest management terms on how to run a business. But at the same time, I realized that it would be very bad for the company if I didn't pay attention to the business indicators.

Doris cites the role of her husband, Jay Christopher, as a significant factor in the company's early growth. Together, husband and wife complemented each other in mentality and in know-how. Jay provided much-needed marketing and management expertise. When the company's growth became explosive, he came on board as vice president of operations in 1987 to supervise product ordering, warehousing, and distribution while Doris focused on working with the growing number of kitchen consultants, which by the end of 1989 had reached 700. Doris recalls how they tried to "do it all" in the company's early years. In hindsight, she is convinced that they should have "brought additional management and expertise to the company earlier."

My husband and I have an interesting partnership. We are very, very different. In the first years of the business, I deferred to his advice. Jay is much more of an entrepreneur than I am. I'm a nurturer. All along the way, he has been a major part of this business with his energy, drive and encouragement. Many times, he has pushed me when I needed a nudge. He has always been very involved in providing financial advice and has been particularly important in long-range planning. He brings to The Pampered Chef extensive business experience that has been gathered from 30 years in marketing and operation positions. He currently serves as the executive vice president of corporate development and in this role acts as a mentor and consultant for the company. Meanwhile, he operates his own business consulting firm.

The Pampered Chef personifies Doris's commitment to the family and her view of dining together as a pillar of family life, with the kitchen as its foundation. While her two daughters were in grammar school, she managed to blend career and family at a time when she was heavily involved in building the business. She worked in her office (at home), doing paperwork, picking out new products and talking to her kitchen consultants. When the girls came home from school, Doris stopped working and switched over to "our time"—when her daughters changed their clothes, ate a snack, and joined her in the kitchen to talk about their day and help as Doris started preparing dinner. She remembers it as a "chance to share some time in a relaxed way as we put the evening meal together."

Even though Doris spent many evenings presenting kitchen shows, the family had at least one all-hands-on-deck dinner during the week and always on the weekend in keeping with her bedrock belief, "When families share a meal, the bonds that hold the family together grow stronger." She always regarded food as a source of extra nourishment: "Food provides a basis for excellent family communication and interaction. If the activity in the kitchen doesn't draw the family in, the food certainly will. Our mission encourages family values."

The mission statement of The Pampered Chef is a business-oriented version of her philosophy: "We are committed to providing opportunities for individuals to develop their God-given talents and skills to their fullest potential for the benefit of themselves, their families, our customers, and the company. We are dedicated to enhancing the quality of family life by providing quality kitchen products supported by service and information for our consultants and customers."

I really wasn't following closely what other companies did. Later . . . I joined the Direct Selling Association [and] started getting lessons at the hands of the master. It gave me ideas on . . . how we could tailor programs that would work for us and our particular company culture. . . .

As the company grew, Doris was transformed from a shopper whom wholesalers indulged to a force in the kitchenware industry all the way back to the design stage. She and her design team keep looking for ways to improve what's out there and to develop products that are exclusive to the company. Innovation is part of her entrepreneuring and key to staying competitive. She came out with the Super Scraper series, whose ingenious design is widely imitated: a spatula head that won't fall off during mixing; silicone construction, rather than rubber, to avoid disintegration and staining; heat-safe to 450 degrees. The result is a scraper that can be used both for mixing batter and cooking in pans over the stove. Her Easy Accent Decorator, which is used for frosting cakes, filling donuts, and creating hors d'oeuvres, has a larger barrel than other decorators on the market. Its one-piece inner construction stands up to stiff frosting, and its soft, comfortable grip allows for one-handed use. She cites these as examples of "making things better rather than cheaper" and of still offering her products at competitive prices.

> *Product ideas come to us in a number of ways. A major source of ideas is our customers and kitchen consultants. They'll say that they need something or want something or ask us why we don't have a particular product. We are constantly checking with our sales people, our hostesses and our customers about what they want. We're always looking for the best product we can offer. Manufacturers will come to us with an idea for a product and ask what we think of it. Based on our research with our customers and our hostesses, we'll say that we will take it or we might ask them to change it to fit our requirements. We're keyed to the functionality of a product. We might ask that a product be made more durable, such as making it out of stainless steel rather than plastic, or that the handle be longer. We are looking for products to be functional, durable, easier to use, to have more features. There certainly are times when we've been less successful than expected with products we offer, but usually our gut instinct is pretty good in identifying a winner.*

In company growth propelled by the "better mousetrap" effect, The Pampered Chef experienced continuous growth by sticking close to Doris's undiluted mission of "providing absolutely excellent products that create meals that bring the family together around the table." By her own recollection, there wasn't time to reflect on what was happening: "We just had time to do what had to be done." Revenues kept increasing: $10,000 in her first three months, $50,000 in the first full year, $200,000 in the third year, then revenues in the millions with sales increasing 4,000 percent between 1989 and 1993.

The growth was fueled by the soaring number of kitchen consultants—from hundreds to thousands—thanks in part to nationwide publicity. In 1990, The Pampered Chef was featured in an article published by *Woman's Day* that provided nationwide exposure. The publicity enhanced the company's image, won attention, and attracted both consultants and customers to the products and the business opportunities offered by the company. The media attention has kept rolling along in magazines like *Family Circle; Success, Inc.;* and *Working Woman.*

Product ideas come to us in a number of ways. A major source of ideas is our customers and kitchen consultants. They'll say that they need something or want something or ask us why we don't have a particular product. We are constantly checking with our sales people, our hostesses and our customers about what they want. . . .

The publicity attracted the key component in direct selling: the people out there doing the demonstrating and selling as the connection between company and customer. Their personalities and style connect with the people at their demonstrations who both enjoy and learn at their kitchen shows. Over the years, the company's kitchen consultants have become a self-selective group that builds company branding and creates loyalty. Doris points out

that the attrition rate for her consultants (a chronic industry problem) is well below the industry average.

> *Our 42,000 consultants, who are all independent
> contractors, are our talent scouts. They're out there
> selling and also finding other consultants. I think that
> one of the reasons our recruiting system works so
> well is that new recruits see somebody actually doing
> the job. They don't rely on an ad and think that this is
> a glamorous job and think they'll try it. They're able
> to see all the good points and the demands they must
> meet by getting real-life exposure to what the busi-
> ness involves. Part of the training for new consultants
> is attending kitchen shows by consultants. If they
> decide to come into the business, they have a
> resource who can answer their questions—the con-
> sultant who recruited them. We support our consul-
> tants in providing that help. We counsel them on
> selling procedures. We make available audio- and
> videotapes on product information and business
> developments. We give them ideas, but mainly we
> rely on the consultants who recruit them. Our sales
> force, which is 99 percent women, has grown through
> one person sharing with another, something that
> women tend to do naturally.*

The result is the army of kitchen consultants who
reflect America's social and demographic trends. They
range from people with full-time jobs who moonlight to
mothers who are supplementing family income. There are
people who are approaching retirement and are building
another source of income; others have already retired.
Overall, most are selling part-time. They do their selling
not only at kitchen shows, but at their workplace during
lunch hour, at trade shows, and at charity fund-raisers.
Some who sell full-time can earn six-figure incomes.

What has struck Doris Christopher over the years is how varied they are.

> *Our kitchen consultants come in all different shapes, sizes and personalities. Some are outgoing and effervescent, others shy and reserved, almost afraid to talk to a group. Some are young and challenging, others older and reserved. It's amazing how all different types are successful in this business. Their own creativity is really what drives them. Their differences contribute to our success. Customers can attend kitchen shows by two different consultants and have two completely unique experiences. I see how unique they are when I travel around the country meeting with our consultants. I see it at our national conference where this year 8,000 consultants came to Chicago—compared with our first conference which had only 35 attendees.*

Doris, who takes pride in encouraging women to become kitchen consultants and thereby entrepreneurs, has found that other mothers discover in The Pampered Chef the work/family opportunity that she pursued in 1980. She points out that they can determine their own hours, set their own goals, and do as much or as little as they want or need to do. One of Doris's favorite examples is a young mother in Georgia, who wrote a letter of thanks. After attending a kitchen show, she "fell in love with the kitchen tools" and took the opportunity to earn free tools by hosting her own shows. Her story didn't stop there. Encouraged by the woman who recruited her, she became involved with the company as a kitchen consultant and, in turn, recruited other consultants.

"The best part," she writes, "is that it didn't take me three to five years to realize a good part-time income and I didn't have to compromise my commitment to stay home. Last year, I struggled to feed my family with macaroni and cheese. Next year, we will enroll our son in private school, thanks to The Pampered Chef."

Similar stories have been told by many other kitchen consultants over the years. The opening chapter begins with a version of Doris's rainy afternoon when she started selling kitchenware. The stories end—thanks to The Pampered Chef—with what amounts to a business of their own.

DOROTHY J. WHITE— MIRACLE SERVICES, INC.

"If You Do a Good Job, Someone Will Notice"

Dorothy J. White—
Miracle Services, Inc.

"If You Do a Good Job,
Someone Will Notice"

One evening in a suburban Maryland home, when Dorothy J. White faced a "jury" of housewives, she had no idea that it was actually her debut as an entrepreneur on the way to becoming president of a multimillion-dollar company. She had been cleaning the house since 5:00 A.M., something she decided to do for supplementary income after her husband became disabled by a heart ailment.

> I worked hard, really hard at cleaning that house. When I got to the house, which was pretty big, I knew I would be there a long time from the looks of how it had been cleaned. I said to the couple who were getting ready to go to work, "I'll still be here when you get back." It took me more than 8 hours to clean that house. I pulled things out from under the couch and bed and from behind the refrigerator. I cleaned and cleaned. When the couple came home, they could not believe what I had done to their home. On top of that, I found jewelry and watches that they probably had

been looking for. "Where did you find that watch?" the wife asked. I told her, "Underneath the oven."

The woman was so pleased. She had never before had such cleaning service. When she asked me how much I charged, I didn't know what to say because I had no idea. I was trying to get a feel for what was out there. So I said, "Just give me twenty dollars." Twenty dollars was enough for me. In 1980, you could buy a lot of groceries for that much money.

But she was shocked. "That's not enough for all this work. I'll ask my neighbors to look at what you've done and find out what they pay for this work. I want them to come over and see what the house looks like." One of the neighbors who came over said, "Oh, my God, would you clean my house?" The woman was paying $45 to a cleaning service and her house wasn't really getting cleaned.

Forty-five dollars was good enough for me. I could clean one house a day. It would take all day, but I would get it done. There were about eight houses in the cul de sac where the woman lived and in no time I had a house for every day in the week. Sometimes, I cleaned on Saturdays, but not on Sundays when I had to go to church. That's how I got started.

What came naturally for Dorothy White is a classic formula for a service business: give customers quality and they will not only become loyal customers, but also do your marketing by recommending you to other customers. Dorothy realized this from the start: "What happened was one person would tell another about the way I cleaned their house and the word just got around." Real estate agents also heard about her. When they wanted a house they had on the market to look spotless, they would call Dorothy. She became known for exceeding all expectations in cleaning a home. It's the only way she has known how to work in building a successful cleaning business. Her operating principle goes back to the home-spun advice she heard while growing up in rural Georgia: "Daddy always said, 'If you do a good job, someone will notice.' "

I used to worry and think, "If only I had a little more education" . . . [But success] . . . has nothing to do with education. It's the way you treat people.

The "good job" has enabled her to build a company—Miracle Services, Inc.—that provides cleaning services throughout Baltimore, Washington, D.C., suburban Maryland, and Northern Virginia with a workforce of 600 full- and part-time employees. The business, which started out with residential customers, is now completely in commercial cleaning of offices and grosses annual revenues approaching $10 million.

Dorothy White's personality, as well as her work ethic, has undoubtedly been a driving force in getting her business to take off. She's a natural salesperson who has the crucial ability to sell herself and also win trust, which was particularly important for the many working couples in the Washington, D.C.–Maryland area. They literally turned over the keys to their homes to Dorothy and left for work. Don't ask Dorothy for a complicated explanation of how this happened. She was just being herself.

I don't know what it was about me. They just saw this honest face. Somebody that they could depend on. I would walk in and they didn't know me from a stranger on the street. They would trust me in their home. For many of them, this was helped by a recommendation from someone they knew. They would go to work and give me the key. So I had the key to all their homes and would go in and clean them. Let me tell you some of these homes were in bad shape. I mean really bad shape, because most of the people had to work and didn't have time to clean. So they needed someone like me that they could trust to come into their homes to clean it well. It was a plus for them. If I cleaned on Saturday, they had to be gone. I didn't want them in the house. I would tell them, "Go shopping, you all have plenty of money. Or go play tennis." That's the kind of relationship I had with my customers. It was like I was a part of their family. And the business just grew from there.

From the start, Dorothy was certain there was a demand for what she offered. This was confirmed at a health club she frequented. She would end up in the sauna, where she inadvertently did "market research." The cross section of toweled women in the sauna included well-to-do housewives who were complaining about cleaning companies that were doing a "lousy job" for them and wishing they could find somebody "who did a really good job." Dorothy knew what she was going to do.

We were living in an apartment with our three kids and I was worried about how we would make ends meet. God, what were we going to do? So when I saw a help wanted ad for cleaning, I told my husband that I wanted to try for the job. He told me to go out and try. When I got to the house, there were four or five cleaning companies already there and I said to myself, "I know I can't compete." The man of the house called me in last. Using my Southern charm and honesty, I said to him, "Look, I know that I'm not a company, but one thing I know how to do is clean. I know I can clean your house for you. If the company you pick doesn't do a good job, give me a call. Here is my phone number."

[Being prepared] is exactly what business is all about. You never know what's going to hit you until you are out there and experience it for yourself. In business, as in driving your car, be prepared for all the other drivers.

Not long after, the lady called me. Evidently, the company she picked didn't do a good job just the way the women in the sauna complained. She didn't say that out loud, but it was clear from the way the house looked. She said that she wanted me to clean her house and that was how I met her neighbors and settled on the $45 I would charge.

After Dorothy's first year, her husband, Jim, who had been a sales manager directing a staff of more than 40 for the company making Royal typewriters, pointed out something that Dorothy never paid attention to. She was starting a business. Taken aback, she said: "A business? What do you mean a business? I'm trying to help make ends meet. I don't know anything about business." She was right on one count: her childhood and years of parenting did not seem to point toward entrepreneuring. On the other hand, her evolution into the Miracle Lady ("I'll go anywhere, any time, to do a cleaning job.") was based on a tireless work ethic and a determination that was just plain built-in. In particular, she demonstrated that when a strong personality meets the right circumstances, an entrepreneur can emerge, though it may not have been recognizable in the little girl in southern Georgia who picked cotton for eight hours a day for $3.

After school, on Saturdays and during school vacations, which they scheduled at cotton picking time, we picked cotton when I was growing up. My mother and father would wake us up very early. It was still dark outside. We had to get ready. The cotton truck would come at three in the morning on picking days and we had to be out there when the truck came by. The cotton owner would stop the truck on the way to the cotton fields, which were about 40 miles away, so we could buy something for breakfast—bologna, sardines, cinnamon buns, cheese. If we didn't have the money, the cotton owner would lend us money. If you picked a hundred pounds of cotton, you got three dollars a day. That would take about eight hours. There was no such thing as machines. You had to pick on your knees and I can tell you it was hot out there.

If you don't have money on deposit in a bank, don't expect that bank to lend you any money for supplies and equipment. After saving and depositing $25,000, we finally got a loan. Before that, I made do by shopping for cleaning rags and for used vacuum cleaners at garage sales.

We were four boys and two girls in our family and we would give what we earned to my mom to try to help out. But you know what she would do? Every weekend she'd give the money back to us. It was ours to spend on whatever we needed, shoes, clothes, whatever. My dad and my mom worked in the cotton mills. The ten dollars he made every week was enough to feed the family. We picked the cotton and they made cloth out of it. I used to go and see my dad working in the mill, loading and unloading machines. He worked there so long with all those machines going that he was hard of hearing. When he came out from the mill, his face, his beard, his hair were all white. He died of emphysema from working in those mills.

My mom and dad worked hard and they kept the family together. We never had what children have today. We made our own toys, made up our own games. At Christmas, we got apples and oranges as gifts and my mother would make a cake. My mother, who's still living at 89, points out to us today that we never complained. She herself can't get over the fact that she doesn't have to use an outhouse now that she has all the comforts, including air conditioning. I say to her, "Mom, we didn't know any better. We were happy."

When Dorothy finished high school, the only work available was cleaning house and that's what she did while living at home with her parents and also while visiting relatives in New York (where she lived with her aunt for several years). It was in New York that she met and married her husband, James, before moving to Columbia, Maryland. When he had to stop working after a triple-bypass operation and Dorothy began cleaning houses, she points out that "the nicest thing was that he was there to help me with running a business." The first step was getting an accountant to handle the books; a friend of her husband came over one evening to start the paperwork. Next, her husband told her she needed a name for her business.

I was cleaning this one house and I was thinking about what to call myself. One of the kids in the family came in with her friends, which I didn't want. I always told my families that I didn't want anyone around while I cleaned the house. One of the child's friends called on the telephone while I was vacuuming and when she heard the noise she asked what it was. "Oh that's the Miracle Lady," the girl replied. And that's where I got the name for my company, Miracle Services.

Armed with a name and guided by her accountant, Dorothy White completed the paperwork and was in business. Raising capital, which she called her "greatest challenge," was still down the road.

One of my neighbors had beautiful handwriting so I asked her to write fliers [that described my business] . . . . My children would go out in the evening and put fliers at people's doors. In the evening, after dinner, I would distribute fliers myself.

If you don't have money on deposit in a bank, don't expect that bank to lend you any money for supplies and equipment. After saving and depositing $25,000, we finally got a loan. Before that, I made do by shopping for cleaning rags and for used vacuum cleaners at garage sales.

To handle her growing business, Dorothy faced a typical growing pain—"getting honest, dependable, hard-working employees." Her solution was to advertise in the newspaper, have people fill out applications, and trust her gut feeling in hiring them. Dorothy started with only three people. She went out with them as team leader, picked them up in a van, cleaned side by side with them, and also supervised them closely. And she set the standard for what clean is by doing the hardest rooms—bathrooms and kitchens.

> *With four people, we could do a house in one hour. Each person would do two rooms while I did the bathrooms and the kitchen. I could do all that and still look around and see what my team was doing. The team stayed together in one house. With all of us working together, we could finish a house in an hour. Then as I added more teams I would name someone that I had worked closely with as leader and I would go around from house to house to make sure everything was in order. It took awhile to get new customers to trust someone else in their home, but they did.*

Dorothy did not rely only on word of mouth to build her customer base to 150 homes in two years. She used fliers, distributed door to door.

> *One of my neighbors had beautiful handwriting so I asked her to write fliers for me that said, "Are you one of those people who are not happy with your cleaning service and would love to have somebody really clean your house?" My children would go out in the evening and put fliers at people's doors. I would also send out my employees on days that we finished early. I always kept fliers in the van so we could put them at people's doors. In the evening, after dinner, I would distribute fliers myself.*
> *I had never been a salesperson myself and it was amazing for me to knock on people's doors. At first, I*

> *just put the fliers on the door knob real easy, but finally I got brave enough to knock and tell them who I was. Most of the time, people would let me right in. I remember the first time I ever knocked on a door. I could hear the family yelling and screaming. I really didn't want to knock, but I was walking around already and didn't want to leave. The husband opened the door and practically yelled, "What do you want?" I said I'm not from the church, meaning the Jehovah's Witnesses who knock on people's doors. He laughed and said, "Come on in. Who are you?" I told him, "I'm the janitorial service." And I got a customer from that house call.*

Miracle Services was still expanding its residential cleaning when Dorothy's "good job" principle worked again. A businessman, impressed by the way Dorothy was cleaning his home, invited her to come to his office.

> *He asked me if I had ever cleaned an office and I said, "No." Still, he said he wanted me to clean his office. So I started cleaning his office and Wow! I found that it was easy compared to cleaning homes. You clean in the evening when there's no one around. It's fast and you're finished in no time. I didn't have to worry about the wife and about personal stuff getting misplaced. Then word-of-mouth led to other small offices in the Columbia area. While I still was cleaning homes, I would go out in the evening and clean a few offices. Not that many to start out with. I could go in and do an office and be out of there. Think of it, what does a small office need? I did it all by myself, cleaning offices by myself, starting out the same way I started cleaning homes.*

She built the commercial side of her business with referrals and office-to-office selling that paralleled what she did with residential cleaning, helped by tutoring from her husband. He would drive her in the family car from one company to another and tell her what to say, what to offer, what to ask. At first, Dorothy was a reluctant sales-person.

> *I would have butterflies in my stomach when I went into these offices. Once I got inside, people didn't want me to leave. They wanted me to stay and talk to them. I'd forget what I went in there for and spent my time talking to them. I'd walk back out to the car and my husband would ask me if I found out about the company, talked to whoever arranged for cleaning, and told him about my services. When I didn't have an answer, he told me to go back in there again. There were so many times that I would have to do that. I'd go back in and say, "Look, I'm trying to get business. I need your help." They would look at me and realize that I had just been in there. But they were so nice. People were really nice to me. So, after awhile, I didn't have any problem going out there and selling. I don't know what it was. There was just something about me that they liked.*
>
> *Education will not do it for you. You know it took me a long time to figure that out. I used to worry and think, "If only I had a little more education." It has nothing to do with education. It's the way you treat people. I've seen a lot of people lose business and I'd walk in and get it. They lose business because of their personalities, the way they act toward others—and some of these people have lots of education.*

To expand her business opportunities, Dorothy began the demanding process of receiving certification for fed-eral contracts from the Small Business Administration's preference program for minority-owned businesses. That led to an $887,500 contract to provide janitorial services for the Social Security Administration in Maryland. Another early contract, won in competitive bidding, was to handle maintenance at the Middle River Depot, a General Services Administration warehouse. Dorothy emphasizes the importance of certification in opening the door to federal contracts. For Miracle Services, it was a major factor in the growth of the company and its transition to commercial cleaning. (In the changeover, she turned over residential clients to her employees.)

> *If you happen to be a minority person or a woman, there are types of programs to help you. Large companies and government agencies are required to contract out a certain percentage of work to minorities and companies owned by women. I advise getting in touch with the Small Business Administration (SBA) to obtain information on how to become certified as a minority company. SBA's 8(a) program for minorities provides for referrals to government agencies for contracts. The process of certification is very time consuming, but it is well worth it. To get certified, you must provide a great deal of personal background and financial information and once you have completed the package, it takes SBA about six months to review the information and make a decision on certification. The 8(a) program has helped my business tremendously and I recommend it for all minority companies.*

One aspect of her operation persists: "hands-on leadership," which Dorothy considers the linchpin of Miracle Services' success. Under her leadership, the company established a track record, drew on a growing list of references and referrals, and signed up both governmental and private organizations—from Westinghouse Electric, Martin Marietta, and American National Savings Association to the United States Departments of the Army, Navy, Interior, and Transportation. During on-site walk-throughs of organizations that were accepting bids, she has overheard her competitors say, "If Miracle Services is bidding on this job, then we don't have a chance." Along with contracts, she has won awards, including Minority Small Business Person of the Year and Administrator's Award for Excellence Certificate (U.S. Small Business Administration), Minority Entrepreneur of the Year (U.S. Department of the Interior), and Governor's Citation (State of Maryland).

Always follow your dream. You should like what you do and be good at it. I tell people that everyone has a gift. If you want to start your own business, you must know who you are and what your gifts are. Then you've got to go out and take the initiative.

Seen up close by her general manager, Barbara Hamilton, who has worked for Miracle Services for four years, Dorothy's business formula comes down to the way she treats everyone—the same. "This makes us all want to work really hard for her. A lot of her success comes from being a caring, down-to-earth person. I've never worked for anyone like her. She cares for everybody in the company from someone in my position down to the janitors that do the work and are the backbone of this company. She'll go into a building at night on her tour of job sites not as the owner and president of this company. She goes in like an everyday person and just goes up and talks to everybody. She knows them by their first name and comes across as very friendly and very caring. She's just as likely to pick up a broom or mop and work right next to them."

Whenever Barbara accompanies Dorothy on a speaking engagement—whether formerly homeless men who have been rehabilitated or troubled teenage girls at a center—she witnesses the charisma that has captivated customers. Only it's heightened. "When she speaks to a group, it's as though she hypnotizes them. It's amazing the attention she gets. She speaks from the heart. She tells them about her growing up, picking cotton, living in rural Georgia, always working hard, raising her own family and then building her business. They listen intently and leave on a high." Barbara has also experienced Dorothy's thoughtful gestures, such as the day she decided impulsively to do something special to show her appreciation for the work done by her headquarters staff of 20. She came in early and, on her own, prepared sausage, scrambled eggs, bacon, juice, coffee, and rolls that were ready and waiting when everyone started arriving at 8:30 A.M. "It was her way of saying thanks for all our good work," Barbara says.

Miracle Service's cleaning staff of 600 presents a special challenge. About 180 are full-time employees working at federal offices where prior clearance is required, thereby limiting flexibility in hiring. The rest are part-time and the object of continuous pursuit and the source of competitive edge, given the nature of the business. Technology is not a threat to the cleaning business, because no matter what innovation comes along, offices still need hands-on cleaning by reliable, careful, and competent people. Wastepaper baskets will always need emptying, floors cleaned, rugs vacuumed, surfaces dusted—regularly. The cleaning company that does it best leads the pack, and the way to do it is with capable employees, which Dorothy White takes as a special concern and a continuous challenge.

Let me tell you how we hire someone for our commercial cleaning. I rent a conference room in a hotel in the neighborhood where our office contracts are located and search out people in the area who are looking for work. They come into the conference room and we have them fill out applications right there. We interview them and then figure out the ones that we think are good. We'd rate them as A, B, or C. Once we hire them, we keep a constant check on how they do, how reliable they are. Sometimes, someone will take a pen or stamps, stupid little things, and we have to let them go immediately. It's a shame. You know this is a tough business, very tough and the competition is intense. You have to stay on top of everything, all the time, and make sure your customer is happy with what you're doing.

A lot of the people that we hire don't even know how to clean. They don't know what cleaning is all about so we hire them and train them. We have rooms at our headquarters to practice cleaning. We have a bathroom where we can show them what to do and what we expect of them. They have to know about tile floors and the different types of floors, about vacuuming. We drive home the way they must work and the responsibilities of going into an office and not disturbing or taking anything.

Looking ahead, Dorothy sees more expansion for Miracle Services as her daughter Maria (currently executive assistant) plays an increasingly important role in the company. She wants to include pest control, mechanical contracting, lighting management, waste management, and security services. Personally, Dorothy wants to share her know-how in dealing with the Small Business Administration to help other entrepreneurs. She wants to offer consultant services and to provide seminars that cover the key business issues that she had to learn as she went along: organization, finance, government, contacting potential customers, human resource planning and procedures, and sales and marketing. Then there's what Dorothy identifies as the "be prepared" component of succeeding as an entrepreneur, starting with the readiness to give the business "your all, 24 hours a day, seven days a week."

> *Going into business for yourself is like getting your driver's licences for the first time. You study hard and you pass both the written and the driving parts of the test and you say to yourself that was easy. You are now driving along in your nice car, staying within the speed limit, and all of a sudden some nut comes along and hits you from behind. You are sitting there, not quite knowing what to do. The police arrive, knock on your window and ask you for your driver's license and registration and you are so stunned by what happened that you have no idea where your license and registration are. This is exactly what business is all about. You never know what's going to hit you until you are out there and experience it for yourself. In business, as in driving your car, be prepared for all the other drivers.*

Underneath the uncertainties and complexities of doing business (which are unavoidable), there is Dorothy White's fundamental business advice (which is necessary for success).

> *Always follow your dream. You should like what you do and be good at it. I tell people that everyone has a gift. If you want to start your own business, you must*

know who you are and what your gifts are. Then you've got to go out and take the initiative. Don't wait for someone else to do things for you, because it's not going to happen. If you start a business, stay in the face of your customers to make sure they're happy and, most important, make sure your employees are happy.

8

JoAnne Shaw—
The Coffee Beanery, Ltd.

"The Best Coffee in the World and Service with a Smile"

JoAnne Shaw—
The Coffee Beanery, Ltd.

"The Best Coffee in the World and Service with a Smile"

After the opening day of a gourmet coffee shop in a new suburban mall outside Detroit, store founder JoAnne Shaw counted her receipts after working hard all day Sunday selling cups of coffee for what was in 1976 a premium price of 75 cents at a time when the 25-cent cup was still around. To open the store, JoAnne and her husband, Julius, went into hock for everything they owned— their house, their cars, and their coffee service business.

JoAnne was delighted when the day's receipts passed $100 and then totaled $120.

Julius was discouraged: "If this is all we're going to do in a day, then we're in deep trouble."

The next morning Julius would be working at an insurance agency to pay the family's bills, and JoAnne would begin her daily one-hour commute from their home in Flint, Michigan, to the coffee shop in suburban Dearborn. Hours were from 9:00 A.M. to 9:00 P.M., seven days a week. The Shaws' all-out venture was built on JoAnne's "commitment to be successful in selling the best coffee no matter what it takes. . . . I was convinced that if people would come and taste a quality cup of coffee, they would come back again and want more." On opening day, it didn't look like there were enough people in the first place.

. . . I attended courses and seminars on making business plans, on management and in areas like public speaking. A business without a leader who has public speaking ability is a difficult business to promote.

"What it took" was JoAnne's 2-hour daily commute and 12-hour days without pay for a year before her commitment showed signs of paying off. She stuck to her conviction that "if we built it, they would come." Her basic business formula was uncomplicated: "The best coffee in the world and service with a smile." The two key ingredients for the coffee are a high-quality bean properly roasted and freshness (no brewed coffee is allowed to stand for more than 20 minutes). For good measure, she has added innovative coffee drinks that appeal to non-coffee drinkers.

After a money-losing and payless first year, JoAnne's formula for what was called The Coffee Beanery started to prove out, reason enough for the Shaws to keep on going. From one store they went to eight in 1985, then moved into franchising on the way to a total of 188 different locations in 31 states. Of the 188, 28 are owned by the company, 138 franchised, and the remainder licensed. The customers keep coming back, spending $52 million to drink 450,000 cups of coffee a week, 23 million cups a year. Along the way, a headline writer dubbed JoAnne Shaw the "Queen of Bean."

Over time, she has customized coffee roasting for coffee aficionados and developed different venues for selling coffee. In her relentless pursuit of gourmet coffee drinkers, JoAnne has customized the different ways by which the company reaches out to customers, adapting and adjusting what has worked for other products. The regional mall store, located in high-traffic shopping centers, accounts for 85 percent of the company's stores. They specialize in selling coffee drinks, whole beans, coffee-brewing equipment, and an extensive line of gift sets. Streetfront cafes offer a comfortable environment for relaxing, reading, and meeting with friends. In addition to coffee, they serve salads, sandwiches, and desserts. Some cafes even have a stage for poetry readings and musical performances. Espresso carts are self-contained 3-by-10-foot mobile units with their own water supply, refrigeration, sink, and refuse container. They offer a range of brewed coffees, such as espresso, cappuccino, lattes, mochas, and dessert coffee beverages. A fourth venue, a kiosk, is a free-standing unit with a full-service coffee bar and food and, often, a select line of coffee beans.

Whatever the venue, The Coffee Beanery goes where the people are, whether pedestrians or shoppers, on the premise that the greater their numbers the greater the chances that they would stop for a good cup of coffee and get hooked. In relying on location, The Coffee Beanery is pursuing customers for the second-largest-selling commodity in the United States. Specialty coffee, the company's main product, is the fastest-growing segment in the industry. The optimum location, as pinpointed by franchisee Virginia Clausen, is "center court in a busy Class A mall."

When JoAnne opened the Dearborn store in 1976 at the age of 32, she was a coffee advocate who became an entrepreneur by marriage and circumstances. Only years later would she ever think of herself as an entrepreneur.

I never dreamt of owning my own business, but I do remember my high school graduation when we heard a motivational speaker who at the end of his speech said to the class, "Everyone stand up." I don't remember the speech, but I do remember the entire class standing up. There were a few hundred of us and he said, "Look all around you. Five of you will be successful and perhaps one will be very successful." That made an impact. I knew I was going to be one of the five. I didn't think through how or why that would happen. I just knew. As to coffee, I don't know what drew me to it, but I love the product. It's a warm, friendly beverage and it really fits me.

It's a process of learning to delegate and of choosing the right people. It requires the skill of learning to let go rather than to hang on. You look for people who have greater skills than you have in many areas. If you can't do that, you can never grow a business.

One thing led to another. While still in high school, she had worked on weekends at a chicken-and-rib restaurant run by Julius and his mother and then married him after graduation. She worked full-time in the restaurant and they started a family (sons Kurt and Kevin, who are now part of the company). On the side, her husband started Ye Olde Coffee Service, a coffee-vending service for businesses in the Flint area. The restaurant closed in 1968, and the coffee service was almost sold after Julius joined an insurance agency. Julius remembers wanting to sell the coffee service: "But Joanne said no. She'd run it. It was something she wanted to do and started doing. But if you had said to me that she'd become a business person, I would have said that she did not have the spark at the time. But she grew into it. Going out and talking to people—from gas station owners to presidents of big companies—got her confidence up."

JoAnne took over the service with its 60 accounts. Each customer was supplied with coffee-making equipment and Ye Olde Coffee Service delivered fresh coffee on a weekly or monthly basis. To attract new customers, JoAnne would demonstrate a coffee brewer, make coffee, and serve it. Her goal was to sell people on coffee.

> *What destroys coffee is being exposed to oxygen. So the coffee we sold in our service was gas flushed. It was protected by a layer of carbon dioxide which is a freshness pillow that coffee gives off at every stage of roasting. The coffee we supplied clients was sealed in little packets protected by carbon dioxide. Each packet made an individual pot of coffee. Our service was full-proof. We furnished offices with restaurant-quality equipment—which most offices didn't have—and pre-packaged coffee. They put a filter in a drip brewer and made coffee. The main thing is not serving coffee that's old, because coffee evaporates after it is brewed and that makes a huge difference in the taste. That's why coffee tastes awful when a place starts with poor quality coffee and then it sits on the burner, evaporating and condensing. It becomes too concentrated. That happens after about 20 minutes on the burner. One of my lines in my demonstrations was "We don't have old coffee, just good old-fashioned service."*
>
> *When I went around to offices to make demonstrations, a lot of people would say, "I love the smell of coffee, but I don't like the taste." I just had the feeling that if we built a place where people could come and*

*experience really high quality coffee, smell it, taste it
and sample it, they would come back for more. In the
1970s, there wasn't a lot of good coffee around and I
had a gut feeling to open a place where people could
taste really good coffee. So we began looking around
for a place to put such a store and happened to come
across a regional mall that was being built in Dearborn. It was going to have 180 stores, five movie the-
aters and an ice skating rink. When we approached
the developers, we offered a store that was different.
They already had any number of shoe, clothing, and
jewelry stores. But at that time in the Midwest, a coffee store was a unique thing. The developers offered a
location. We were pretty naive. We said "OK, if you
think that's best for us." They named a rent and we
said, "OK, if you think that's fair." They said sign on
the dotted line and, we did, for a ten-year lease.*

. . . [At] my high school graduation
. . . we heard a motivational speaker
who . . . said to the class, "Everyone
stand up." . . . There were a few hundred of us and he said, "Look all
around you. Five of you will be successful and perhaps one will be very
successful." That made an impact. I
knew I was going to be one of the five.

---

*After we left the office, we looked at each other and
said, "I think we'd better get financing to build the
store." We didn't have it, but the leasing agent
assured us that it wouldn't be any problem. He sent
us to a friend whom he said was a banker. He was in*

downtown Detroit. We went up something like 22 floors and were ushered into this man's office. It was one of those offices where his desk and chair looked like they were six feet off the floor and we were three feet off the floor. We told him what we planned and what we wanted and he asked if we wanted a partner or a banker. We said we had each other for partners so, of course, we wanted a banker. At that point, he was called out of the office by his secretary. When he came back, he leaned over the desk and said, "I'm not interested. Goodbye!"

Thus began the entrepreneur's familiar merry-go-round in search of financing, toting financial documentation and statements and a description of the enterprise in the making. It took six tries, determination, and a tough skin to overcome the treatment they received. When they went to the Detroit bank that was financing the mall, the bank officer told them they didn't have the collateral for the $50,000 they wanted to borrow. Another banker in Detroit put his feet on the desk and bluntly dismissed them, "You've got champagne taste on a beer budget."

Next came the banks in Flint where the Shaws soon realized that they faced a Catch-22 situation. The bankers in Detroit resisted lending money to out-of-towners, the banks in Flint resisted lending money for an out-of-town enterprise. On their sixth attempt, the Shaws prevailed upon the bank with which their coffee service did business. (Many of its branches were also the service's customers.) The commercial loan bank officer relented only after everything from the coffee service to the Shaws' house and cars were put down as collateral and after the Small Business Administration (SBA) provided backing for part of the loan. To get SBA approval, as recalled by Julius, JoAnne worked hard at "putting together all the paperwork, including the numbers, by hand. . . . Staying with it and getting it done was a lot of work. Without it, we wouldn't have gotten the loan. It was a crucial point, because without the loan we wouldn't have opened our first store." Today, based on the experience of her franchisees, JoAnne reports that borrowing is not as difficult because The Coffee Beanery stores have a successful track record. "But it still isn't easy to get financing."

Building the store was the next hurdle.

> *We had a friend and neighbor who was an architect and he designed a pretty good store for the first time out. Never having built a store in a regional mall, we were not prepared for the amount of time that it was going to take to get it built and get it opened. As it was, we missed the grand opening of the mall. Before our own opening, we needed a name. I made a list of 60 names and showed the list to friends, relatives, and employees at the coffee service. We kept weeding down the list until we came to The Coffee Beanery. It is very descriptive of exactly what we do. We are a coffee store and we sell coffee beans.*

I just had the feeling that if we built a place where people could come and experience really high quality coffee, smell it, taste it, and sample it, they would come back for more. In the 1970s, there wasn't a lot of good coffee around and I had a gut feeling to open a place where people could taste really good coffee. . . .

> *Because it was the Pepsi Generation and people were accustomed to sweet drinks and not accustomed*

to quality coffee, I created some dessert coffee. The first one was called "Hot Spice Viennese" and I worked on it in my kitchen so it would be ready before the store opened. I played around with trying to make a coffee drink that was quick and easy to make and tasted really good. I wound up creating a spice mix to add to the coffee. To provide a familiar taste, I added some liquid chocolate to the coffee—which, of course, was brewed. The combination was topped with whipped cream.

After building and opening the coffee store, I had to run it. It was then I realized what a passion I have for the business. I liked going to the store every day. It smelled wonderful. The customers were fun. You found out what the regulars liked and you could kid with them. We steadily built the business in the first year, adding other products and selling house blends of coffee beans. We created in the first store a signature coffee called Beanery Blend. It has a bit of a snap to it that comes from the way we blend the coffee, which is a secret. The blend is still a best seller in our stores.

As the first store became profitable, the Shaws' entrepreneurial spirit stepped up. The Shaws went into partnership with the architect who had designed the store. Together with the Shaws, the architect and his wife opened another mall store in the Detroit area. Its success further confirmed JoAnne's formula. A few years later, the architect's marriage broke up and he faced a divorce, complicating the partnership with the Shaws. The choice came down to buying the couple out or selling the store to them. They were bought out and then the Shaws planned a third Coffee Beanery in another mall.

The Shaws were plugging into the mall phenomenon. Malls were being built throughout the United States and attracting hordes of customers, thereby providing ready-made traffic from which to attract coffee drinkers. Husbands of shopping wives were particular targets. "There is a theory that men don't like to shop, probably 90 percent of them," JoAnne says. "They may not mind their wives shopping, but they like to take a break and have a cup of coffee while they wait for their wives."

By the time the Shaws planned a third mall store, the time came to make the decision to throw their lot in completely with coffee. The coffee service and the stores were becoming too much to handle while Julius continued to work at the insurance agency. So he quit and devoted himself to running the coffee service while assisting JoAnne in store operations. With successful stores in tow, the problem of satisfying the bank requirements for collateral disappeared. It also was time for the next move—franchising—something that JoAnne dreamed of doing to win more coffee converts.

> *I'd always wanted to franchise. I liked the idea of helping other people get into business. I like teaching them and working with them to give them an opportunity to succeed. Franchising is a chance for people to be in business for themselves, but not necessarily by themselves. After we had eight stores and were in business for nine years, we began to look into franchising as an opportunity for expanding our business and taking it beyond the Michigan market.*
>
> *I was really nervous at the beginning. Actually, our first franchisee was someone in another system. He bought one of our units and made a commitment to open a second unit. He helped us get started in franchising. From there, we found a location in another Detroit-area mall that was going to open and advertised for a franchisee. That's what we would do. We'd advertise for franchisees in local newspapers when we found a promising location in a particular area. We also set up booths in franchise shows and joined the*

International Franchise Association through which we did a lot of franchise marketing.

. . . We needed a name [for our business]. I made a list of 60 names and showed the list to friends, relatives and employees at the coffee service. We kept weeding down the list until we came to The Coffee Beanery. It is very descriptive of exactly what we do. We are a coffee store and we sell coffee beans. . . .

I really like to see women get involved in franchising. For the most part, the women I've gotten involved with in franchising work very hard. I find them putting in long hours and being very devoted to what they do, including the nuts and bolts of the business. One example is Virginia Clausen who worked with me in our first store and put in even longer hours than I did to make it a success. She left to have her first child and then a few years later I talked her into coming back to work for me. We found a location in Grand Rapids and I knew that if there was a way of getting her over there that the store would be a success. By that time, she was divorced with two small children. So I went into partnership with her with the goal of eventually having her buy me out. She invested the $20,000 she got from her divorce settlement and with my investment plus a bank loan was able to fund the store in the Grand Rapids Woodland Mall. Four years later, she bought me out and now has a second store—and a second husband. She has won our

"Manager of the Year" award twice and the "Best Customer Service" award three years in a row from the Woodland Mall. When you meet people like her, you just want to help them make a success.

JoAnne has built into the company culture a people-first policy that includes the franchisees as well as customers, such as the time a new franchisee who had just opened called frantically to company headquarters. Her coffee grinders, she reported, were not working—no grinders, no coffee to brew and sell. Rather than send a repairer or even ship a replacement grinder, JoAnne sent her son Kevin to the scene of the problem with a replacement grinder. As it turned out, the franchisee needed some more instructions on using the grinders, which were in working condition, after all. Kevin took care of the situation and flew right back, leaving a happy franchisee. On another occasion, JoAnne filled in for a franchisee couple on opening day when the wife needed emergency surgery and the husband needed to be at her side. JoAnne minded the store.

One of JoAnne's most successful franchisees goes back to The Coffee Beanery's opening day in Dearborn as a customer. Diana Dimitroff, then a recent graduate of Michigan State University, became a triple convert. Already a drinker of supermarket coffee, she discovered gourmet coffee when she went into the shop. She also was won over by JoAnne's "warmth, energy, passion for quality coffee and the way she made you feel at home in the coffee shop. It was like being a guest in her home." On top of that, Diana started to think about opening a coffee shop of her own. It took 13 years of staying in touch with Diana, saving enough money while working in a sales position, and waiting for the right location. As with JoAnne, a new mall in suburban Detroit provided location and Diana became The Coffee Beanery's 31st franchisee.

By then, Diana was well prepared, starting with a careful self-examination to see "if this is what I wanted to do." She had added a master's degree and then took extension courses on starting your own business that included personality evaluations and seminar discussions on what it takes. The courses introduced her to the realities of financing, incorporation, taxes, partnerships, and advertising. Her advice to others planning to start a business is "Do it, if you feel in your gut that this is what you want and need to do. Do it while you have the chance." When the time came, Diana had saved enough money, thereby avoiding the need to get a loan which she knew would be "extremely difficult, especially for a single woman without other visible means of support."

After building and opening the coffee store, I had to run it. It was then I realized what a passion I have for the business. I liked going to the store every day. It smelled wonderful. The customers were fun.

To anyone considering the franchise route, Diana advises: "It should be something you enjoy doing because you're going to spend a lot of time learning the business, tending to it and keeping things going. If you don't like it, I don't see how you can spend so much time on it. Certainly, as with any business, you need to look at the numbers, talk to a lot of people in similar and different businesses and, in the case of franchises, visit and talk to other franchisees." Diana identifies labor as the most difficult problem: "getting quality individuals who can do the job, training them and keeping them."

For JoAnne, in her process of evolving from young wife helping in the family restaurant to store operator to president of a far-flung coffee enterprise, it was a matter of growing to match the challenges. She epitomizes the life-long learner who develops skills and know-how to meet growing responsibilities.

I'd always wanted to franchise. I liked the idea of helping other people get into business. . . . Franchising is a chance for people to be in business for themselves, but not necessarily by themselves. After we had eight stores and were in business for nine years, we began to look into franchising as an opportunity for expanding our business and taking it beyond the Michigan market.

I don't even have a college education. I never had the time for it because I got married at 17. What I've done is take business courses and seminars, meat-and-potatoes learning that has been very advantageous. While running the stores, I attended courses and seminars on making business plans, on management and in areas like public speaking. A business without a leader who has public speaking ability is a difficult business to promote. With the help of really wonderful coffee people around the world, I've become a coffee expert. My husband and I have traveled a lot for coffee—to Guatemala, Costa Rica, Honduras, El Salvador, Jamaica and Hawaii. We have a lot of relationships within the coffee world and in some cases directly with farmers.

We've actually developed and trademarked our own Right Roast system so that each of our coffees has a different roast that brings out the special qualities and nuances of the particular coffee bean. Depending on the bean, the roast can be light, medium or dark. Also, you have to adjust to whether the beans are early, mid- or late crop. We're constantly examining coffee samples and roasting the beans to make sure that we have the right roast for the particular coffee. Green brokers, as they're called, ship us the samples for testing and we then order coffee through them.

JoAnne cites her Right Roast system as a differentiator in matching up with her best-known competitor, Starbucks, which she describes as having "a different product and a different image."

Starbucks is a really high quality company and they have expanded the market in a very good way by highly training their staff and maintaining consistency and quality in their product. I like competitors in the market that are good. It makes us sharper and better and makes us work harder. Starbucks is different from The Coffee Beanery. It looks down on flavored coffee. For instance, we have Cafe Carmel, which has become extremely popular and people walk into Starbucks asking for it. Also, all of their coffee is dark roasted whereas we have Right Roast which varies roasting according to the particular bean. We have everything that Starbucks has and we have choices, in addition. We do everything they have and we have better coffee.

Always ready to innovate by borrowing or inventing ideas, JoAnne is on continuous alert. She cites The Coffee Beanery's initiatives in concocting dessert coffee drinks and selling frozen ice coffee slushes. For three years running, a "Lucky Mug" was a big seller. JoAnne designed a four-leaf clover and printed the design and a name on it as a good-luck gift. "Something," she says, "which came out of my mind, probably at three in the morning when I get my best ideas."

One thing people tend to do is limit themselves in their own minds. Perhaps they don't have as good an education or the credentials other people have. . . . If you stretch yourself and do some of the things you're challenged to do, you'll find the abilities. They will come along with the opportunities.

As the franchising expanded, JoAnne faced the successful entrepreneur's need to delegate, part of making the transition to business executive.

It's a process of learning to delegate and of choosing the right people. It requires the skill of learning to let go rather than to hang on. You look for people who have greater skills than you have in many areas. If you can't do that, you can never grow a business. It's a big adjustment, but you must make it.

But you also run the risk of making the wrong choice and taking a licking. It can set you back years. At one point, we made a mistake in our choice of chief operating officer. He was a fairly long-time acquaintance and had been giving some good advice along the way, but when I brought him on board, he had a management style that was based on intimidation. It created problems with our employees and with franchisees. The one thing that I can say about this person is "Not as advertised." Once on board, the personality that I didn't recognize became clear. It was his way or the highway whereas we operate by consensus, which is the way I think that most women manage. The mistake set us back three years, the two years he was here and an additional year.

JoAnne learned familiar lessons when enterprises hire key people. First of all, good consultants don't necessarily make good managers. Secondly, make certain that new hires fit company culture. When husband and wife are partners, a formula for success includes a division of responsibilities, a separation of home and office, a yin-and-yang balance, and the ability to work differences out. In the case of JoAnne and Julius, their match is made for success. "I tend to be the optimist, the dreamer, the visionary; he tends to be more pragmatic," JoAnne says. Julius agrees: "I would call her the visionary of the company. I'm the realist. Behind every good woman, there is a good man who keeps everything on track. Sometimes I have to reel her back. She'll talk of having 2,000 stores and it's great to think that way, but when we sit down to do strategic planning, we have to think realistically about where we want to be. Every once in awhile JoAnne gets upset at me because she says that I'm too much of a pessimist. I say that I'm not a pessimist. Being a realist is a lot different. I always try to follow a 24-hour rule. Don't make a final decision until you think about it for 24 hours."

JoAnne's sense of humor flavors her version of how they "work fairly well together:"

We've been married 37 years and not only do I work with my husband, I work with my two sons and I

> *also have franchisees. There must be a place in heaven reserved for me. Actually, he's a really super guy and we balance each other in a lot of ways. Certainly, he asks questions that make you grit your teeth, but they're good questions. I know a lot of people say they could never work with their husband or wife, but there are advantages to it. Certainly the trust factor. It's nice to know that if you're not in the office that he's going to handle things the way they need to be handled. He's very involved in the financial portion of the business, which provides a real comfort level for me. And he brings a different view to things, which is very important. Do we have power struggles occasionally? Sure. But we resolve them. It's no big deal.*

Julius recalls that JoAnne's publicity value as company president was clear from the start: "When we started 21 years ago, we knew that a woman president would give us more publicity because then there were even fewer women running companies. The Beanery is her baby, the Coffee Service is my baby. Her baby's gotten a lot bigger than mine, but we still manage to keep our feet on the same path and keep moving in the same direction. She's the president of the Beanery and I'm the president of the Service. JoAnne and I each own 41 percent of the whole business, the boys own nine percent each."

After working together with JoAnne, Julius has a set of guidelines to share with any other husband-wife entrepreneurial team:

- Keep an open mind. "You really have to be able to talk things through with each other."
- Never go to bed mad at each other. Remember as husband that "you can always have the last two words in the conversation: 'Yes, Dear.' "

- Keep the business away from your home life. "That's tough because you're in your business 24 hours a day, seven days a week."

No one is better qualified to assess JoAnne's winning ways than Julius. When asked how he would fill out the "Accomplishments File" that The Coffee Beanery maintains for all of its headquarters staff, he provides a close-up of his wife the entrepreneur and a template for all entrepreneurs. "She's good with people. She's well-organized. She sets her goals and pursues them. Sometimes, she's like a bulldog. Once she gets her mind set on something, she goes right for it. Damn the torpedoes. Full speed ahead. She provides a powerful marketing advantage for our stores and our franchisees with her involvement in the worldwide coffee industry and her extensive public relations efforts. She's been president of the Specialty Coffee Association of America and twice has been a featured speaker at the World Coffee Symposium in Vienna. She is going to become the first woman chair of the International Franchise Association. That was a big goal for her and she stayed with it, bucking the old boy system. All the while, she's been able to see the big picture and stay open-minded."

When JoAnne and Julius look to the future, they run true to form. JoAnne can visualize 2,000 franchised locations. Julius sees 300 to 350 locations, still an ambitious outlook, but in keeping with what he views as his realism. Then, as on opening day of the first Coffee Beanery store, Julius looks at the numbers and focuses on the bottom line: "Anyone in the world would want to buy in, if they enjoy the business and the business is profitable."

JoAnne the entrepreneur and visionary deserves the final word.

One thing people tend to do is limit themselves in their own minds. Perhaps they don't have as good an edu-

cation or the credentials other people have. But I think the Good Lord takes care of those things in the long run. If you stretch yourself and do some of the things you're challenged to do, you'll find the abilities. They will come along with the opportunities. For me personally, the biggest thing has been the coffee business and my passion for it.

9

SHARON LOBEL—SEAL-IT, INC.

"I'm Always Thinking About Different Ideas to Try"

SHARON LOBEL—SEAL-IT, INC.

"I'm Always Thinking About Different Ideas to Try"

In 1986, the founder-president, purchasing director, sales manager, shipping clerk, and receptionist of Seal-It Tamper Evident Bands, Inc. (now just Seal-It, Inc.) operated out of the guest room of a suburban Jericho, Long Island, home. A bed was in one corner; in the other, an improvised desk was loaded with typewriter, telephone, fax, and calculator (no computer). The phone was answered with "Good Morning (or afternoon). Seal-It, can I help you?" Sometimes the calls came from Asia, sometimes from the next town. If Sharon Lobel (who wore all of Seal-It's hats) were there, she dealt directly with the caller; if she were out grocery shopping, the answering service responded as if it were part of the staff, took a message, and promised that "Sharon would call back."

To this day, some callers ask, "Does Sharon still work there?"

As Seal-It's founder, Lobel now runs a company with annual sales of more than $20 million—projected to exceed $100 million in five years—but her business card still has no title on it. "At one time, I was the entire sales force for Seal-It. Today, even with six sales people,

175

including a national sales manager, I continue to work directly with several customers and some don't know I'm the company president." She still works close to 12 hours a day, five days a week, and stops by on Saturdays, except that now her executive desk is at Seal-It's current location in a 100,000-square-foot space in Farmingdale, Long Island. Some 160 employees are turning out tamper-evident seals and plastic packaging for 1,000 customers, including such global companies as Coca-Cola and Du Pont. Seal-It's slogan speaks for itself: "You'll feel better if it's sealed better." As the founder and builder of the business, Lobel views herself as an anomaly, not because she's a successful woman entrepreneur, but because of the way her current manufacturing business started.

A manufacturing company is not normally started from home. In my case, I had the idea, the customer base and knew the business, but I didn't have the financing so I started from my home and imported my products. Today, thankfully we are seeing progress in women being able to obtain financing to start new businesses. But from a business point of view, I never focused on being a woman. I always looked at myself as a person who went into business. Sometimes women go into things and start out with a negative feeling that they won't be able to do something because of being a woman. I never look at anything that way. At trade shows, many times when people come to our booth with a technical question, they will ask one of my salesmen, assuming that as a woman I wouldn't know the answer. Such is life. If that makes them more comfortable, I'm fine with it. I don't have a problem with it. I've never even thought about it. As long as we get the order, it's okay with me. Over these years, I've been recognized not as a woman, but for my achievements in the industry as a manufacturer.

When asked by a trade publication to name the businesswomen she admires most, she shrugged off the gender-based question and answered (without realizing it) with a mirror image of Sharon Lobel: "I admire a type of businessperson rather than a particular businesswoman. The type of person I admire is someone who takes something from nothing and is able to build it up. This person can be a man or a woman. Specifically, among the people I admire, is Oprah Winfrey. From humble beginnings, she built an entire empire. In order to achieve that type of success a person has to have self-confidence. You have to believe in yourself and not give up. Don't let obstacles stop you. If you can achieve that, it may be your greatest success. Conviction and self-confidence are vital."

My best skill is selling. I thoroughly love selling. It's what I always wanted to do.

At Seal-It, Lobel has built a home-based, one-person company into North America's largest supplier of shrink-bands, plastic labels, and plastic packaging in a marketplace that boomed after the 1982 nationwide scare when seven people died from poisoned Tylenol capsules. Fear, paranoia, and legislation created a demand for drug and pharmaceutical products whose packaging would make tampering evident to the buyer. The industry was improvised overnight with importing of tamper-evident materials from Taiwan and Japan, where the technology was developed. Lobel's company started by supplying that demand by importing the material; manufacturing came later.

In the 1990s, a new dimension was added to her business: colorful, graphic packaging that sells as well as protects. In the years since the narrow niche market of heat-shrinkable tamper-evident bands exploded after the Tylenol episode, demand for shrink-bands has expanded across supermarket shelves, from mustard to mascara. Lobel's company has been right there.

> *Our business started by supplying tamper-evident packaging, but now color and design are just as important. Originally, 95 percent of our business was on the antitampering end. Now it's maybe 50 percent, with the other half labels, multi-packs and combination plastic packaging. Since the Tylenol scare, many people have gotten used to seeing tamper-evident seals on a wide variety of products, from pharmaceuticals to food. So much so, in fact, that the lack of a seal can raise consumer concerns. I remember buying a container of pretzels and noticing when I took it home that there was no tamper-evident seal. I was afraid to use it. But it's not just me. Other people have told me that if a product doesn't have a tamper-evident device on it, they're not comfortable. Was there a band? Wasn't there a band? Should I use it? Shouldn't I use it? If the band is there, it gives you a feeling of security that no one was there before you.*

Lobel's company now manufactures and markets in an industry that is a complex web of technology: Asian and U.S. manufacturers, highly competitive suppliers, specialized know-how, customized machinery, demanding customers, and product specifications as precise as a single strand of hair. Lobel's success is much more than a matter of opportune timing. She combines, as the epitome of an entrepreneur, business savvy, people skills, drive, energy, self-developed know-how, and total immersion in her business. She has pulled it all together—the right people, machinery, products, and customer relations—in an industry whose pace and complexity belie the simple (and often frustrating) struggle to get shrink-bands off an aspirin bottle or a six-pack. What she calls "the necessary evil," tamper-evident merchandise, brought opportunity to her suburban home.

> *For companies that bottled vitamins and pharmaceuticals, suddenly having to deal with suppliers of neckbands was a problem because the manufacturers were all in Asia and the U.S. suppliers were not that responsive. That's when I realized that there was room for a locally based, customer-friendly supplier of these seals. At the beginning, pharmaceuticals and vitamin companies took the lead with tamper-proof bands. Soon afterward, the food industry became more aggressive, even though there are no laws requiring the food industry to have these bands. Supermarkets began to dictate the bands, telling companies that they won't get shelf space if they don't bring in products with tamper-evident devices. So more products have jumped on the bandwagon. If you walk into a supermarket or in a drugstore, every time you go in, there are more and more products that are using this packaging for a lot more items besides food and pharmaceuticals. We're doing a tremendous amount now with cosmetic lines. Every eyebrow pencil, every lipstick, every mascara has a clear band with a laser code on it. Overall, the market is still growing. I think that it's still in its infancy.*

The tamper-evident bands are polyvinyl chloride (PVC) in tube form. They slip over a container and pass through a heat tunnel, which shrinks them on. If the seal is broken, it is immediately evident to the consumer, making the bands *tamper-evident,* the quality that's been in high demand ever since the Tylenol episode. Though, as Lobel points out, "nothing is completely tamper proof," it makes the products "virtually tamper proof." Once a bottle is opened, PVC bands break and can't be put back together, unlike wet bands which resemble them, but haven't gone through a heat tunnel. As a result, when put under running water, they expand and then shrink back without evidence of tampering. Even pull-up tabs can be glued down without evidence of tampering.

Lobel points out other factors that are adding to the industry boom and her company's prospects—waste reduction, shelf appeal, and protection against customer chicanery.

Follow your dreams. If you feel you want to do something, go for it. People give a lot of advice, but you have to do what you feel is right.

The overall growth of the heat shrink industry can be traced to the emphasis on reducing packaging waste. In the past bottles were usually packaged in paperboard, in addition to carrying a label, which was quite costly. Today, a shrink-wrap band provides a combination of tamper evidence and graphic appeal which allows it to stand out on store shelves. In cases where shrink bands were once used as tamper-evident caps, the entire label can now be a shrink sleeve, with a perforation around the cap, still providing tamper evidence. Even items like sporting equipment are carrying a shrink-wrap band to provide tamper evidence. Take basketballs, for instance. Retailers faced a problem with customers who would switch boxes, placing higher priced basketballs in lower priced packages. But when a shrink band is used, the band remains with the product. Once off, it's off for good.

Looking back, Lobel started with a mind-set in search of the right opportunity: "I was always very interested in business and always thinking about different ideas to try." But don't look for family influences that directed her toward entrepreneurship: her father was a cab driver, her mother a dressmaker. She started to develop sales and marketing savvy as an assistant buyer at Bloomingdale's, having dropped out of Queens College after less than two years as a psychology student. She was bored. She also worked for an optician who had a chain of stores; when she left after two years, she was running the business. "People thought I owned it." As a suburban housewife, she sold clothing from her home, ran charity events, and started a company that sold plaster crafts in Korvette stores and closed when Korvette closed down.

Her education in the flexible packaging industry began as a part-time bookkeeper who soon became assistant to the president of a company that packaged no-name vitamins for its customers and put their label and a tamper-evident band on the bottle. The bands were a bottleneck, bought through an uncooperative U.S. supplier who was difficult to deal with. So Lobel was commissioned to set up a subsidiary to manufacture tamper-evident bands. She plunged into the project with the expectation of getting a piece of the business. It didn't work out and she came out of the project empty-handed, except for an education in the industry and a renewed determination to start her own business: "I was ready for it. I was more mature than when I tried starting a company selling plaster crafts. My daughter was away at college. I was ready to do something."

She quit her job cold and spent three months setting up a business to import Asian-made packaging materials as a supplier who was determined to be customer-sensitive. "My best skill is selling. I thoroughly love selling. It's what I always wanted to do." With the guest room as her office, the basement became her sample room for local customers. She ordered stationery, drew up a brochure, lined up suppliers in Taiwan and Japan, and by using as collateral property she owned with her engineer-husband, established a line of credit. By day she pursued customers by phone, by night she dealt with her Asian connections (because of time differences).

> *You know it takes a lot of energy and time to start a business. Many people think you go into business and everybody does things for you. Not at all, you work twice as hard and twice as long. I did a lot of phone work. I had tons of lists. I followed up many leads. Talk about work. I was working 12 to 15 hours a day. I got up early and sat on the telephone all day calling different people, different contacts. Then at night until 10 or 11 o'clock—morning for them—I was faxing to the Orient the details of what I wanted. You had to spell everything out. There was at least a nine-to-ten-week lead time for delivery. God forbid it came in wrong. You had to start all over again. That was a nightmare.*

A manufacturing company is not normally started from home. In my case, I had the idea, the customer base and knew the business, but I didn't have the financing so I started from my home and imported my products. . . .

When the material arrived, I'd take it to the garage, check everything as quality control, pack it and reship it. Gradually, the business took over the basement and the garage as well as the guest room—but not the living room. At that point, as a middle person I was caught between cash flow and making sure the material was right. Remember, if you ordered a yellow printed band and it came in orange you were in trouble. One advantage I had in avoiding costly mistakes was in hiring an English-speaking Taiwanese engineer who worked in this country before moving back to the Orient. Someone I knew was his very close friend and led me to him. He became the eyes and ears of the company in Asia. He worked for us, overseeing everything that was ordered. Nothing shipped out from Asia without his signature of approval. That helped me tremendously.

So it went for the first stage of Lobel's business—importing the printed neck bands and labels and shipping them to her customers ready to heat shrink around their products. She made a profit from the beginning. After four years, she had annual sales of $1 million, growing expertise in the industry and a good-sized, loyal list of customers. (Ninety-five percent of her original customers are still with her.) Thanks to her job experience and to her widespread networking, she had access to customers and knew what they needed. To win customers over, she had an edge with her appealing customer-first approach in a field not known for customer-friendly service. She's certain that she succeeded from the start because she has always offered the "best possible customer service, trying in every way to satisfy customers, never saying no to what they needed and always going all-out to help them." In addition, because of her working arrangement with the Taiwanese engineer, she was able to negotiate favorable terms with Asian producers and thereby put a competitive price tag on high-quality products.

But there was no more room in her guest room/basement/garage operation. It was time to expand by finding a financial partner who was right for her, particularly someone who would let her keep control of the business and run it her way, while making it possible to expand. In the search for several potential investors, Sharon learned an important lesson in picking partners. From the first contact, trust is paramount. She compared what potential investors wrote in a letter of intent with what they said when they sat down to talk. When their spoken words didn't match their written words, which were legally binding, they failed the *trust test*. She ruled them out as a potential partner.

You know it takes a lot of energy and time to start a business. Many people think you go into business and everybody does things for you. Not at all, you work twice as hard and twice as long. I did a lot of phone work. I had tons of lists. . . .

When she met her current partner, Ron Nasser, through a business contact, everything "clicked immediately." In Nasser, a successful international art dealer with galleries in the United States and Europe, she "couldn't have found a better person." She trusts him "110 percent" and the feeling is mutual. He personally had the financing to invest and he also opened the door to financial relations with the Israel Discount Bank, with whom he has close relations. Seal-It has worked closely with the bank ever since and between the bank and Nasser, the company has never had any problem getting the financing that's needed.

In 1990, the happy partnership was launched with the June opening of a 5,000-square-foot Hicksville, Long Island, warehouse with one cutting machine and four employees. This enabled Seal-It to import tubing in rolls and to cut it to customer specifications. The company could also produce samples. But in a matter of months the business demanded further expansion. Lobel was ready to become a manufacturer, which meant printing labels in her own facility.

> *By the end of '90, I decided that this is not going to work if I'm going to grow the way I want. We were still importers. Big customers want to work with somebody who's printing neck bands and labels in this country. Also, I am a control kind of person and I wanted to have total control here. I didn't want to have to be dependent upon somebody across the ocean. So I realized that I have to do my own printing. So by the end of the year, I had a six-color press on order. And believe me—everybody, but everybody— tried to talk me out of doing this. They said start small—buy a one- or two-color press—don't go in so deeply. But I felt this was the right way and I had to do it the way I think it should be done. That was my first press.*

In no time at all, she was proved right. Seal-It continued to grow. Next stop was a 50,000-square-foot facility with more people and more machines—cutting machines, slitters, seamers, and, most important, its six-color printing press that set the company apart from the competition. In the first five years after moving out of the guest room, Lobel's business grew at an annual rate of 80 percent as Seal-It offered the twin appeal of shorter cycle time and greater customization. One enthusiastic customer, who was dealing with importers from Taiwan for thousands of printing variations a year, raved over the Seal-It difference. Lead time of 12 to 14 weeks was reduced to 5 weeks. After the six-color press came the seven-color press (plus four more presses) and the latest, an eight-color press, which Lobel singles out as "more high tech" than anything the company has done before and making Seal-It a "pioneer in the industry."

Everything we do is custom ordered. I go to people who know the technology and I work with engineers to put together a press. . . . I've been in the packaging industry for a while and know a lot of people. I look for whatever people are willing to teach. I'm more than willing to learn.

Lobel, the indefatigable salesperson, turns enthusiastic techie in describing a specially designed press that uses flexography, whereas the rotogravure process is standard in the industry. The press prints on a diverse range of plastics and has required the development of special inks. Of about 10 companies selling shrink-bands and labels, half are importers, and among those that do their own manufacturing, Lobel reports that her company is the only one in the United States using modified flexographic printing. She points to Seal-It's inventory—$2 million of cost-effective generic PVC material—and its ability to produce pull tabs, horizontal and vertical perforation, and shrink-bags in 12 different shapes. On top of that, Seal-It can come through with delivery as quickly as two days to two weeks. When she talks technology, she sounds like a car buff who has put together the best and fastest customized car on the block.

It is really incredible, this eight-color press. It's 70 feet long, a monster! Actually, it's nine different presses made into one. The press has automatic splicing, can unwind and rewind. If I put a job on the press, it can run for four days and I never have to shut it off. The press automatically takes a roll off and puts the next one on without stopping. I had the idea, I knew what I wanted to do. I certainly didn't have the technology to know how to build a press so I worked with people who, in turn, worked with engineers who had the expertise we needed. After the first press, my current director of operations came aboard and he was able to design each generation of press so that it was an improvement on what went before.

Everything we do is custom ordered. I go to people who know the technology and I work with engineers to put together a press. Remember, I've been in the packaging industry for a while and know a lot of people. I look for whatever people are willing to teach. I'm more than willing to learn.

You know when you look at a piece of plastic, it looks like absolutely nothing. But I can't tell you the technology involved and how technical that band is and how precise it must be. We send out labels in tube form to big accounts like Tropicana and Heinz with a tolerance of half a millimeter. That's less than a pen line. If I'm off by an extra half millimeter, the shipment is garbage. I could do the nicest printing job, but because the big companies apply the plastic wrap with automated equipment, their specs call for incredible precision.

To get the word out on Seal-It, Lobel has mixed advertising, public relations, and trade shows, expanding her efforts in each area as company facilities expanded and business increased. To build credibility, her ads feature the lineup of major customers with instant recognition, such as WD-40, H.J. Heinz, Clorox, Coca-Cola, Johnson & Johnson, and 3M. In the 1990s, an active PR effort produced articles on business pages, in trade publications, and in magazines such as *Success* and *Working Woman.*

. . . Two years ago we had two new presses on order that had not arrived in time to do labels for a huge dairy. We gathered all our people together. . . . They worked every single Sunday and were working around the clock with the presses we had on hand just to make sure that the customer wasn't disappointed. . . .

When Sharon Lobel is asked about her product, the salesperson in her comes to the fore as she compares paper and plastic: "Who would want a paper label when you can get plastic? It's so much more vibrant. The coloring and the art that you can do on a PVC shrinkable label is so much more vibrant than the coloring you get on paper. If you put one next to the other, there's no comparison."

At the same time, she's aware that her company's product is not run-of-the-mill for her customers, particularly small businesses. "This is not like buying a chair or a table. It's an odd type of item. We walk clients through the whole process to make it easier. The clients run the gamut from small Southern hot-sauce makers to Tropicana."

To respond to the range of customer needs, Sharon set up a customer-focused sales operation, which she regards as the best in her industry. She has staffed it with experienced salespeople strategically located throughout the United States and has set up her system so that regular customers always call a person they already know, either in the field or at headquarters. Salespeople in the field team up with counterpart service reps at headquarters to serve the same customers. Sharon reports that this customer knowledge not only serves current needs, but can update customers on new technology and even anticipate future needs.

Whatever happens at Seal-It, Lobel is in the middle of it. It's what she unabashedly identifies as her "personality," a paradoxical combination of hands-on and hands-off, of constant involvement and complete confidence in her management team, of being unmistakably in charge and of thinking of the company as "we" rather than "I."

> *I'm a control type person; that's just my personality. I know everything that's going on, even now that the organization is all set up. I have wonderful managers who have really contributed to our growth. I have a great crew here, very good people that really care and work as if it's their company. It is in a way because we all grow together and our success benefits everybody. But, I still know what's going on; that's just me. I'm not one to say, "Okay, now all the managers are in place. I'm going to go out and play golf." That's not my personality. I'm here. And I do run around all the time and I do know everybody by name in the factory and I do know what jobs are on the presses. Everything we do, we do as a group.*
>
> *To give you an idea of how we work, two years ago we had two new presses on order that had not arrived in time to do labels for a huge dairy. We gathered all our people together and we said, "Look, until all these presses come in, we need your help to meet this order. We don't want to lose the contract. We've got to supply them." Well, they worked every single Sunday and were working around the clock with the presses we had on hand just to make sure that the customer wasn't disappointed. Another time, a customer came*

in with a rush order that had to be in Pittsburgh by the next morning at 5 a.m. We pushed hard to produce what was wanted and then our quality assurance manager rented a U-Haul, drove through the night and delivered the order by 5 a.m.

I'm always thinking about the business. I compare it to the way parents think about their children. No matter where you are, you're always thinking about your children. . . . If you leave your kids with a babysitter, your mind is always still on them. . . .

Our employees have a sense of pride in what they do. When we get a new client, everyone is as excited as I am. When inventory time comes and we have to work 20 hours a day, they're all here willingly. I've been asked why I keep my business in Long Island when I could move to the Carolinas or Alabama and pay half the expenses I do now—but I could never duplicate the work force. My original factory staff is still with me. In New York we are very aggressive. People move quickly and have the attitude of "It's got to be done now." But being on Long Island we have a softer tone than in New York City. I want my employees to know that they are a large part of this business. I always tell them I could never have done all this by myself. Despite the high cost, staying here has always worked for me and as the saying goes, if it's not broke, don't fix it. Besides, this is my home. I've been on Long Island since right after I got married and my married daughter has bought a home here.

Adds her director of operations, Al Brancaccio: "She works very hard to make people feel like it's a family operation here by knowing everyone by name, asking how the kids are doing and even bringing in lunch for everyone once a month." (On a Thursday in July, it was 35 large pizzas for the day shift, followed by similar deliveries for the other two shifts in her 24-hour operation.) Lobel recruited Brancaccio, a veteran of the industry who runs the Farmingdale facility and puts in as much time on the job as she does. He combines the basic Seal-It recruiting requirements: experience, enthusiasm, and expertise.

Other recruits like the print manager ran a large printing company; the head of production managed the warehouse and part of a converting facility for a packaging company; the controller ran the accounting department for a large manufacturer of medical products; the marketing manager worked on Madison Avenue and also for a competitor; the quality assurance manager was trained in Europe and has worked for major U.S. and European companies. Lobel personally recruited them for a company where no one works harder than the founder-president whose first employee, Therez Shepard (now in charge of sales for the New York area), describes Lobel as the same as when she started with her in 1990 with the opening of the Hicksville location. "I don't think she's changed much. She has the same energy and attitude, except that in the beginning everyone wore so many hats. After awhile, she's had to delegate and let go of certain things. One thing she always has done is make everyone feel like an integral part of the company, including the workers in the back. With customers, we get lots of requests to help solve packaging problems. We never say no. We explore all the possibilities. That's part of our immense growth in the industry. We don't limit ourselves. If we didn't come along, you wouldn't be seeing shrink wrapping on so many different things. The one thing that comes to mind about Sharon is that she is very hands on. When someone doesn't show up for work and we need to get something out, Sharon will go back on a cutting machine."

Husband Robert, Sharon's wholehearted supporter from the start, describes her as someone who's absorbed in whatever she's doing and always doing her homework. Before buying her first cutting machines, as recalled by Robert, himself an engineer, she did "tons of research, talked to all sorts of people," asking: What is the best machine to use? Which ones provide the best quality? Which are fastest? Her philosophy to this day, he notes, is to do extensive research on any machinery or equipment she's going to buy. Even before she began buying machines she went to trade shows on machinery. When asked why, because such shows had nothing to do with her business at the time, she replied, "Eventually, it will." When she started to own machines, her husband would stop by after his day's work to make adjustments on the machines or handle such tasks as changing the blades on a cutting machine. She was at his side learning how to do it herself.

In recalling what it was like at the beginning of Seal-It, Robert chuckles. "How much did we talk about the business? Every single night." The focus still never stops: "She just loves her work and puts everything into it. I can't tell you how many times she will think of something on a weekend," he reports. "It can be at nine or ten o'clock on a Saturday night and we'll run over to the office to work on it to get it ready for Monday. Or if it's two or three in the morning and we get a call from the overnight shift about a problem with the presses or some other thing, we're right there. Everyone has our home number and knows that they can call here." When the Lobels go away on vacation, Robert heads for the golf course in the morning while Sharon spends the first two hours of the day talking to the office (and again in the evening, if need be).

The people she hires catch the spirit—or they don't

stay. In her hunt for the right staffer, she's unrelenting and in screening them, she lets them know what the company culture is like.

> *I find prospects through contacts, through talking to people I know in the industry and weed out the people who are not right for us. In a job interview I'll tell people that we're a wonderful company to work for—we really are—but it's not the company for everybody. You must have the right mind set, not be a nine-to-five person who wants to get out right on the dot of 5. It doesn't work here. I'll ask them what their last job consisted of. What was their day like? What did they do all day? And then I'll tell them—not only the good things here, but also the long hours, the craziness, the juggling of work. Everything is a priority. It's not the kind of place where you come in and say, "This morning I'm going to do this and this afternoon I'm going to do that." You're probably going to juggle 20 things and whatever you planned on doing, you're going to do 10 other things. When people hear what the job entails, you can tell a lot from their facial expressions. That maybe it's too much. Some people start with us and it's just not right for them or it's not right for me. We part ways and I'm sure that they're successful somewhere else. But when we get the right person, he or she is here for good.*
>
> *Working here, everybody really puts in a lot of time and effort and really cares about the company and that's important—plus the way we do everything together. I don't sit back and say this is exactly the way we're going to do something. We have meetings, we talk about it. We have managers' meetings where everybody gives their opinion. I continuously talk to people on the plant floor. Who knows better how something runs than the person who's doing that job?*

Ask Sharon Lobel about doing her own job and out comes a description of a nonstop day, lunch at her desk while doing paperwork, her office door always open with staffers lined up outside to see her. "It's called the bakery line," reports Therez Shepard, the first employee hired by Sharon. "Five or six people are lined up to talk to her— from the warehouse with suggestions, from the sales people checking a quote, from the press room asking about a deadline."

But she's hard to pin down at her desk. Her employees describe her as "always on the road" for her walking-around style and her direct contact with everyone who works for her. "Yesterday," Lobel notes, "the men in the press room complained to me, 'How come you didn't stop by yesterday?'" From the time she arrives in the morning until she leaves in the evening, it's total immersion for Lobel by her own play-by-play account:

> It's hard to describe my day. I could have 20 more things added that I never planned. It's a full day, nonstop. I never take lunch, except at my desk—unless a customer comes in. I come in at 8:30 or 9:00 and I never get out of here before 7:30. When I get in, I go into my office and work on quotes. I make sure all the pricing is done. Then I talk to the customer service people because everything comes through them. Then I talk to my director of operations and our coordinator who follows all jobs through to completion. I'll walk around, make sure everything is on schedule, visit the finishing area where we do quality control. Later in the day I'll see how shipping is doing. Sometime I'll get stopped so many times that it will take me four hours to get to the warehouse. We don't necessarily talk business. We may talk about their families, about what's going on in their lives. Then there's all the paperwork I'm doing. I used to do a lot more, but I've

given up quite a bit. I have an open-door policy in my office and that takes up an enormous part of my day.

For anyone wanting to follow in her entrepreneurial path, Sharon packages her advice in a compact set of guidelines:

1. Come up with an idea.
2. Get the right financing.
3. Make sure it's the right time of your life.
4. Research what you're doing "very, very carefully."
5. "You have to feel it. You can't do it just for the money."

Then she adds the entrepreneur's trademark determination: "Follow your dreams. If you feel you want to do something, go for it. People give a lot of advice, but you have to do what you feel is right."

Like an inner voice that never leaves her, the entrepreneur in Sharon Lobel is always there. Ideas pop out anytime, anywhere: new types of packaging to provide customers, new customers to convert to the advantages of plastic packaging (such as the company that ordered shrink-wrapping for satin hangers), new machinery to buy, new companies to acquire (such as a plate-making company for the printing operation). But all ideas are directed to and viewed in terms of *the* business.

I don't know why my mind works differently than somebody else's. I could be doing 100 things or driving the car and all of a sudden something comes to me. Then I stop and think about it or I'll think about it at night. There are times I'm sitting and doing paperwork and all of a sudden, things pop into my head. I do all the trade shows, which is something that I really enjoy doing. I get to meet my customers and it gives me a whole other perspective of everything. You take in ideas, information. You'll see something and that rings a bell and makes you think of something else.

I'm always thinking about the business. I compare it to the way parents think about their children. No matter where you are, you're always thinking about your children as they're growing up or if you leave your kids with a babysitter, your mind is always still on them. Well, I'm always thinking about my business because this is my baby.

There's something else—Lobel is having a great time. "You know how I do it? I love it. I love what I'm doing and if you love what you're doing and you enjoy it, you can do it. It's not work to me, it's fun. When it's not fun it's the day for me to stop. But I really love and enjoy what I'm doing."

Ebby Halliday— Ebby Halliday, Realtors

"We've Made Service Our Priority"

EBBY HALLIDAY—
EBBY HALLIDAY, REALTORS
"We've Made Service Our Priority"

In 1918, eight-year-old Ebby Halliday rode her pony, Old Deck, from one Kansas farmhouse to another selling Cloverine salve at 15 cents a can, making "very good profit." Each can cost her only eight cents and she had no overhead. "My little pony was my office and he cost nothing to maintain. He ate grass in the fields and spent his nights there." Her door-to-door technique for selling the popular home remedy was plain, simple, and loud. She hollered to farmers in the field or their housewives doing the wash out back: "Here I come with my Cloverine salve!"

Eighty years later, Ebby Halliday, the one-time Cloverine seller on horseback, is chairman and owner of a Texas-size residential real estate firm which has $2.5 billion in annual sales. It is the largest in the Dallas–Fort Worth area, as well as No. 1 in Texas and 16th in the nation among all independent residential real estate brokers. Her army of 975 associates working out of 24 offices earned the firm's latest rankings by participating in 13,002 transactions in 1997. Ebby Halliday, Realtors handles housing for individuals as well as relocation of executive and management transferees of entire companies—with Ebby still in the middle of the action answering her own phone and always on tap to help close a difficult transaction.

Nonstop—for 80 years—Ebby has always been a salesperson. In high school she graduated from Cloverine to a part-time afternoon and weekend sales job at a department store in Abilene, Kansas, where she boarded out since her farm home was 18 miles away from the available high school. Her hollering days were over. "I learned to sell and to relate to people and I learned that the customers are always right, whether they were or not." The Ebby style was emerging, not as someone who sells by pushing and pressuring, but as someone who focuses on the customer rather than the product. Her style has become the mantra of Ebby Halliday, Realtors: "We've made service our priority."

From all accounts, she is the ultimate persuader who succeeds by identifying what her customers want and need and then delivering. Along the way, she has become a Dallas icon who has received practically every civic award Texas has to offer. Her celebrated billboards have been reminding everyone who's ever driven on a Dallas–Fort Worth highway: "You're in Ebby Halliday Country."

What has made Ebby such a success? A first-hand report is provided by Mary Frances Burleson, whom Ebby describes as her clone and who is now company president, 40 years after starting as a part-time Kelly Girl. "Ebby is the product of her background and the environment in which she grew up—the Depression, which was certainly a great motivator. Somehow, her genes must have played a part. She's very ambitious, very capable, and a great salesperson. She listens to people and finds the motivator—the honey spot that works. And she knows her business. She's a voracious reader, understands what's going on and knows how to read people. She can charm the birds out of the trees. When people in town ask me if she's for real, I tell them that *yes she certainly is.*

> . . . I have looked upon every job as an opportunity. I've always looked upon work as a privilege and that's why I'm still at it. . . . There is nothing else I want to do.

"I often say that Ebby's a Pied Piper. People follow her. She doesn't mind working a lot of hours and doing whatever it takes to get the job done. Nowadays, a lot of people are more interested in shorter hours and benefits. But if you're going to be successful you can't watch the clock or the calendar. Ebby has led the rest of us to think that anything is possible. And by golly, it is! Just about anyone who has done anything around Dallas–Fort Worth knows Ebby. When they meet me, they invariably tell me to say hello to Ebby. That kind of recognition is a door opener in our local market to get listings and make sales. So the Pied Piper also has a key to the lock."

In a videotaped tribute to Ebby, an amused (and awed) Dallas executive described his own experience with Ebby the irrepressible Realtor. In 1988, in the depths of the real estate slump in Dallas, he was transferred out of town. As soon as his transfer was announced in the newspapers, he received a call from Ebby at 7:30 in the morning, asking, "May we sell your home?" In three and a half weeks, despite the slump, Ebby's team sold the house and he left town with Ebby's parting reminder, "When you come back to Dallas, we'd like to find you a home." Eight years later, when a Dallas newspaper announced his return, the executive's wife received a phone call at 6:45 in the morning.

It was 85-year-old Ebby calling. "She's offered to find us a home," the stunned wife reported to her husband. His reaction was, "That's Ebby!"

If we are unethical or inefficient, if we make derogatory remarks about others, we injure ourselves. If we share what we are and what we have, we build up ourselves and others and inevitably the whole human race improves.

When a prominent Dallas attorney is asked to sum up Ebby, he settles on one word: "energy." (Back in high school, her hyperactive style as a cheerleader earned the nickname of "Pep.") "When she comes into a room," the attorney says, "you have the feeling that Ebby's here, now we can start." Leading figures in the Dallas community have acclaimed Ebby Halliday as a brand name, and the woman behind the name has been characterized as Dallas's greatest citizen. Summing up her reputation in business, a long-time Dallas businessman, William Fair, Jr., says, "I've never heard a bad word about Ebby."

When Ebby talks about the success of her company, she calls it a "team effort, not a one-woman show . . . I may be the cheerleader, but it's been a team effort." She has built her company by selecting, retaining, and rewarding outstanding managers, by building pride in a home-team approach, and by recognizing the importance of the agents who represent the company.

Admit it or not, Ebby is the highly visible leader of Ebby Halliday, Realtors, starting at 8:30 every morning as one of the first to arrive for work. No important decisions are made without Ebby and that, from all reports, is the way her office managers and brokers want it. In the highly competitive field of real estate, she has combined energy and charisma with a sure sense of what sells and by developing the visibility that attracts both buyers and sellers. She has thrown herself into civic activities not for any applause, but because she's the genuine article—a grassroots farm girl committed to being a good citizen. Inevitably, this counts heavily with home buyers and sellers who are, as property owners, concerned about their community.

When Ebby discusses her long-running career as entrepreneur and civic leader, she counts her blessings and highlights her work ethic rooted in a hard-working, no-nonsense childhood. After her father died when she was 18 months old, Ebby and her brother and sister went to live with their grandfather, a circuit-riding Baptist minister. Their lives revolved around church, Sunday school, and prayer meetings. "We had a good moral grounding and we ate lots of chicken wings at the second table on Sundays." When Ebby was seven, her mother married a Kansas wheat farmer who was an athlete and wanted Ebby and her brother and sister to excel in track meets and at country fairs (at which many blue ribbons were won). In between, the children got up at six in the morning to do chores on the farm before school, more chores after school, then they did their homework and helped around the house.

> *I look upon myself as a very, very lucky person. I've been so blessed. Good health. Humility. Ability. Inspiration. A strong desire to share. I'm very grateful for the genes that my parents bestowed upon me and for the work ethic which I developed. If you didn't work, you didn't eat. Having worked since age eight, I have looked upon every job as an opportunity. I've always looked upon work as a privilege and that's why I'm*

still at it. They say that nothing is work unless you'd rather be doing something else. There is nothing else I want to do.

I've also been fortunate to have been in the right place at the right time in my business career. At $10 a week, I went to work right out of high school for a national millinery company that leased space at the big Jones Department Store in Kansas City. The company transferred me to Omaha and then to Dallas in 1938. In those days, transfers for men were uncommon and practically unheard of for women. To a farm girl in the thirties, Dallas was paradise. The city was still in the throes of celebrating its centennial two years before. Big name performers and bands were still coming to Dallas. There was a great spirit in the town and the mayor had declared the end of the Depression—which was good news to me because I hadn't known anything but the Depression since graduating from high school the year the stock market crashed. Dallas was a revelation of the glamorous side of life and for me it was also full of opportunities.

It was at the W. A. Green Department Store as manager of the millinery department that Ebby made friends, attracted customers, and accumulated $1,000 with a view to opening her own shop. She was still a long way from what she needed to open a shop—when she overheard a conversation between her doctor and his nurse about investments. When Ebby asked the doctor's advice as to what to invest in, she was brought up short. He told her, "I don't advise women." She asked why. He replied, "If they lose, they cry." Ebby said, "Try me." He did, advising cotton futures. She followed the advice, which enabled her to parlay her $1,000 investment into $12,000 in a year.

It was what she needed to open her own hat shop and bring her customers and friends along. One day a customer relayed a message from her husband who had purchased the Walnut Hill Golf Course on the north edge of Dallas and had invested in a new experimental type of housing called Incem (insulated cement, which was touted as the building material of the future). The message was: "If Ebby can sell you those crazy hats, maybe she can sell my crazy houses. Ask her to see me."

Ebby took up the challenge. On her first visit to the houses, she saw cement everywhere—foundation, floors, walls, ceilings—52 Incem houses sitting there unloved and unsold. Even the FHA had withdrawn their loan commitments. She looked at the cement houses and immediately went to work decorating them. Living rooms were converted into early American settings, bedrooms took on a French provincial look, kitchens became homey backdrops for apple pie baking in the oven. The cement disappeared.

One after another, she decorated the 52 cement houses so they looked and felt livable as homes. Her first customers were two shotgun-toting men headed for the nearby open fields to hunt for rabbits and doves. They didn't get past Ebby who greeted them, showed them around the model houses, and made two sales on the spot. "Instead of game," Ebby recalls, "they went home with contracts for two homes. Their wives couldn't believe it." She sold all 52 houses in nine months: $7,500 for two-bedroom houses, $9,000 for three bedrooms. (By the 1990s they were selling for well over $100,000.) The experience turned Ebby toward houses instead of hats.

I didn't stop until I sold all the cement houses. I loved it! So in 1945 I sold the shop and moved out into the Walnut Hills Shopping Center in North Dallas and rented an office. My first salesperson was the wife of one of the hunters who bought the first two cement houses. In my wildest dreams, I could not imagine where the business would go. I didn't plan it. It just grew. I concentrated on selling one street at a time. It's an exciting business. I've always gotten the same thrill and the same satisfaction I got in selling my first two cement houses. You get lots of self-satisfaction in placing people in a home or selling a home when the owners are ready for a change. You fall in love with each family you help.

Ebby's timing couldn't have been better. With the end of World War II, Johnny came marching home and a house of his own dominated the American dream he brought back from the war. As in the rest of the country, residential housing boomed in Dallas and so did the city. When Ebby started selling real estate in 1945, Dallas was a city of 400,000. The Dallas–Fort Worth area reached 1 million in 1961 and practically tripled in the next 20 years.

By the early 1990s, Dallas was first nationally (in 1992) in attracting new manufacturing companies, new plants, and plant expansions. It was second in corporate relocations and fourth in creating new jobs. It was thriving as the financial and commercial center of the Southwest, a city where companies were relocating their headquarters in the oil, gas, insurance, and banking industries, a city whose economy flourished because of oil refineries and diverse manufacturing, particularly in aircraft and electronics. The bigger the boom, the more people and the greater the needs for homes. Both individuals and companies, with their entire cadre of executives and managers, were moving into Dallas–Fort Worth—*Ebby Halliday Country.*

When you're dealing with the transfer of a corporate headquarters, a lot of additional care, know-how and expertise are needed for the families being transferred. Getting the family settled into a new community can be a problem unless the family is happy. We had one woman looking to relocate who had horses. She hadn't found a place for them so we arranged for one of our associates to board them while she found a permanent place. Another family was reluctant to move because their boy was a starting player on his football team. So we helped him get on one of the local teams our company sponsors. I remember one of the first corporations we moved to Dallas. The chairman of the board was a single person who was bringing his widowed sister and her four children to live with him. They loved to play tennis. Well, I found him a beautiful house with 20 acres and they built a couple of tennis courts, which they kept very busy.

Ebby has combined her enthusiasm and drive with the personal quality of the business of real estate and the community-oriented culture of Dallas and Forth Worth. She has been tireless in working both for the community and the real estate industry, and everything she has done has created civic and business benefits. In action, she epitomizes what it means to act locally and think globally. Or, in practical terms, the better things are in Dallas, the better it is for real estate.

Ebby tells a down-home farmer's story that sums up what she is all about with her realistic idealism as a successful entrepreneur whose success in business is tied inextricably to her community service.

We had a neighbor on the farm in Kansas—George Robinson—who had the finest corn in the county. He won the blue ribbon at the county fair every year. When he harvested his crop, he always gave his neighbors some of his prize-winning corn for seed. Someone asked George, "Why do you give your prize seed away?" Uncle George replied, "My neighbors must grow good corn to insure the quality of my crop. The wind carries the pollen and if my neighbors have inferior corn, my own fields will suffer." And so it is. If we are unethical or inefficient, if we make derogatory remarks about others, we injure ourselves. If we share what we are and what we have, we build up ourselves and others and inevitably the whole human race improves.

In Dallas, Ebby Halliday fingerprints still turn up everywhere: in pollution control, business development, and a string of arts and charity organizations. Even her sponsorship of boys' baseball teams in North Dallas has benefited her business. "At least three times I have walked into the headquarters of a company to ask for business in transferring their personnel," says Ebby, "and a young executive has said, 'One reason we called you is because I used to play on your baseball team.'"

. . . [Real estate is] an exciting business. I've always gotten the same thrill and the same satisfaction I got in selling my first two cement houses. You get lots of self-satisfaction in placing people in a home or selling a home when the owners are ready for a change. You fall in love with each family you help.

Two operating principles stand out in her success as a Realtor—going where the business is and maintaining high visibility. She has always been on the lookout for areas where real estate activity is stepping up or about to. Company president Burleson describes that sixth sense as "uncanny." She checks with Ebby before opening a new office and while Ebby usually goes along with her recommendation, Burleson remembers the time she recommended a new real estate office in an area where housing construction was underway. Ebby told her the time was not ripe. It was too soon. Six months later, when Burleson came back with the same recommendation, Ebby gave her the go-ahead. The time was right, and it became one of the company's most successful offices.

Ebby has stayed on top of housing trends in the Dallas–Fort Worth area by dint of her extensive and continuous involvement in the area's business and civic life. In the process, she has been a trailblazer for women: first woman president of the venerable North Dallas Chamber of Commerce, past president of the Greater Dallas Planning Council, first woman to be named Realtor of the Year by the Texas Association of Realtors, inductee into the Texas Business Hall of Fame. She has led the way in bringing women into the real estate industry, not only by her success but by her staffing policies. When she first started, women were a rarity in real estate, possibly 10 in the Dallas–Fort Worth area, and they viewed it as something to do in their spare time. "Now," Ebby points out, "it's a full-time job and then some." In Ebby Halliday, Realtors, 82 percent of the headquarters staff and brokers are women and Ebby sees women and real estate as a natural fit.

> *Women's volunteerism has helped to build this community. Women have provided the threads, the fabric of our city. They have built the human part of our educational system, our health facilities, the parks, art, music, theater. Women are very caring and concerned. Their sensibilities and sensitivities pick up nuances that are easily overlooked. In our business, all this is often an asset.*

Ebby runs her business as "a large company, but a family." One of Ebby's vice presidents, June Feltman, who joined the company as a broker 28 years ago when it had only four offices, can't bring herself to leave. "Two years ago, I told Ebby I wanted to give up managing one of our offices so she asked me to come to headquarters as a vice president in charge of projects. I thought I'd be working part-time. I keep threatening to quit and I just can never quit." She describes Ebby as "infectious" and the company as a "Ma and Pa operation," despite its expansion to hundreds of brokers. "Ebby comes from the entrepreneur of yesterday who cared what each individual customer thought. She has never kept herself removed from any of her associates or from the public. She is always there. We still operate person-to-person as we did before. I have a strong loyalty to the company and I'm convinced that our sales associates do, too. When new agents participate in our training program, we have a luncheon for them and Ebby is there, getting to know every one of them. They can see right away that she is touchable. She has a great sense of humor. I think that's another reason why she's so admired and really loved by her people. And when she gets out her ukulele, then the ice is broken."

June was referring to what has become an Ebby trademark: her ukulele playing. It goes back to her high school days when "everybody played a ukulele." Her current ukulele was presented to her by her late husband, Maurice Acers. He noticed her beat-up ukulele from high school days and decided to surprise her with one made specially for her by the leading ukulele manufacturer in Hawaii. Her ukulele playing became yet another example of how Ebby adds to her image and popularity and to her name recognition by doing what comes naturally and spontaneously. After addressing a sales meeting or a civic group, Ebby whips out her ukulele and strums a tune with lyrics aimed at her audience, which leaves them smiling and remembering Ebby.

The ukulele has a special connection to her late husband, whom she married in 1965 after a seven-year courtship between two very busy people, a lawyer in

Austin and a Realtor in Dallas. As to the couple, "They were quite a team," according to Betty Turner, Acers's executive secretary for many years. "Theirs was a 35-year romance, full of love and accomplishment and doing for others. Everything about this dynamic duo was unusually exciting. . . . certainly their honeymoon." The honeymoon became a company legend. A planned weekend in Mexico City for the two of them turned into a week with 12 people—Ebby and Maurice, his Austin CPA and wife, his Beaumont CPA and wife, his secretary and her husband, Ebby's Dallas CPA and wife, and Ebby's secretary and her husband.

> *We all congregated in San Antonio for the honeymoon and boarded a Braniff 707 to the accompaniment of mariachi Mexican music. When the* Mexico City News *interviewed us at the races that amazing week, we were asked, "Do you always travel with such an entourage?" Our reply was: "Only on honeymoons and big business deals!"*

The years that followed the marriage were growth years for Ebby Halliday, Realtors, with Acers as legal counsel and chairman of the board. An executive committee was set up to make decisions, backed up by department heads to implement decisions and highly trained associates to assist sellers and buyers. The company forged forward in spite of the economic debacle of the mid-1980s. "When many other companies were selling, franchising or merging, Ebby Halliday stood steady," said Paul Hanson, 38-year veteran of the company and its executive vice president (also Ebby's brother). New offices were built, other companies acquired (notably Ellen Terry, Realtors, affiliated with Sothebys), new technology was adapted, and recruitment and training given high priority. Meanwhile, Ron Burgert, company comptroller, made sure the company remained solvent even during the days of massive foreclosures in real estate. Ebby describes Acers, who died in 1993, as "the love of my life, a great man who left big tracks, many good deeds. Our entire organization respected and admired him. An even greater surge of business and civic and political activity helped me cope with the loss."

Our company name is well known and we're proud of it. When people see our name tag, they start talking real estate. . . . At any cocktail party, any social gathering, any public event, the conversation eventually turns to houses. . . . That's why I want my people to wear their name tags all the time.

Ebby has kept her company highly visible, beyond the standard real estate practice of advertising in local newspapers. She has used the exposure offered in such publications as *The Wall Street Journal* and various magazines. She started the firm's own television show, which provides visual tours of homes for sale. Her billboards have become a fixture in the Dallas-Fort Worth area. A state-of-the art web site has been established. Her associates wear company badges that contain their name and the web site address, with varying badge designs and colors denoting sales accomplishments. Ebby makes a point of checking that her Realtors are wearing them all the time.

A favorite story, which reenforces company culture, dates from the time she saw an associate without her badge. "Oh, my dear, where's your badge?" Ebby said to her. Thinking quickly, the woman came up with the punch line of what has become an office joke: "I left it on my night gown." The ever-present badges epitomize Ebby's indefatigable selling strategy aimed at maximum visibility. The wider she and her company cast their net, the more business they will catch.

> *Our company name is well known and we're proud of it. When people see our name tag, they start talking real estate. You'd be amazed. At any cocktail party, any social gathering, any public event, the conversation eventually turns to houses. It's wonderful. That's why I want my people to wear their name tags all the time.*

In building her business, Ebby has emphasized that real estate is a full-time business, with no room for part-time, which Ebby defines as "eight to six in real estate." She has built a total-commitment attitude into her entire operation, going back to her early years when she began with four associates on staff. ("They came to us.") Within a year there were four Ebby Halliday offices, each started "after we found a good person and manager and then looked for a good location." In particular, Ebby looks for brokers who have "empathy" for their clients and see themselves as dealing primarily with a family rather than just selling a house.

As for Ebby, no two working days are the same, though the basic elements are always company, community, and the real estate industry. In an understatement, she describes herself as a "hands-on person," which leaves out the part about nonstop entrepreneur and activist.

> *I get up no later than six in the morning. If I'm going to the office, I leave the house at eight. I drive to the office on the tollway which gets me there in about 12 minutes. It's faster than the local streets. I'm one of the first people to arrive in our corporate headquarters where*

we have about 50 people in a free-standing building of about 25,000 square feet. If I have early-morning meetings with a civic group, I go there first. Sometimes the meetings are at 7:30 in the morning. Once in the office, I read my mail, answer phone calls, respond to the many "good" letters we receive. At least 98 percent of them are addressed directly to our agents. I would be untruthful if I didn't say that once in awhile we get a letter that is not complimentary. We always address those letters. Then I talk to the different department heads. Our other departments are located in the corporate headquarters—training, relocation, bookkeeping, computer services. I'm very close to our PR/advertising department and we have been fortunate through the years to be placed before the public on a consistent, regular basis—over 100 publicity exposures in print each month. Our company does so much in the community, thereby meriting the publicity.

I attend sales meetings and training sessions where I either make major remarks or introduce guests. Then there are business lunches, civic meetings, afternoon appointments with builders, agents and clients. Evenings involve community functions so that at most I'm at home only three or four times a week.

Always thinking ahead, Ebby is planning for the twenty-first century, with Burleson designated to lead the company, backed by the direct involvement of Ebby's people in an Employee Stock Ownership program. Burleson, who has absorbed the Ebby Halliday approach, sums up the business as "very much a contact sport—people want to do business with someone they know, like and trust. Sometimes our associates will sell to the same family four or five times. So forget the national advertising. If buyers and sellers like you, they want you to work with them, their parents or their grown children."

The business outlook is on the company's side. Estimates for the 1995-through-2005 decade project Dallas–Fort Worth as the leading U.S. metropolitan area in gaining both population (900,000) and jobs (400,000). And Ebby Halliday intends to stay in the middle of the action. "I hope to die with my boots on, doing something for my family, my business family, the real estate industry and the community. I would like for my tombstone to say, 'She did the best she could.' "

SHERRIE MYERS— LANSING LUGNUTS

"We're Creating Memories for People"

SHERRIE MYERS— LANSING LUGNUTS

"We're Creating Memories for People"

On a blustery Tuesday evening in December, a couple in their late thirties sat at a secluded table in an Italian restaurant in Evanston, Illinois, engrossed in a winter conversation about baseball, specifically the minor-league team they had bought with the help of investors. They had a problem. All their money was tied up in a Class A team that had languished in Waterloo, Iowa, was limping along in Springfield, Illinois, and was going to move—with bright prospects—to Lansing, Michigan. But Tom Dickson wasn't ready to leave his high-paying advertising job to handle the Lansing start-up. He needed someone to run it.

"What about hiring so and so to do the startup?" he said at dinner. As he mentioned possible candidates, he wondered aloud which came first, business or baseball know-how in executing a complicated triple play. After leaving Waterloo, the team was going to play out a second of two seasons in Springfield while doing the groundwork for a move to Lansing. The year ahead, 1995, would be both phase-out time in Springfield and start-up time in Lansing in preparation for the 1996 season.

Tom remembers Sherrie Myers's blank stare. She remembers thinking that the choice obviously was business before baseball and of saying to herself, "I'm a start-up person with a successful track record. I happen to have a break between startups. I can do this." To be fair, Tom didn't think of Sherrie, not because she would be a woman in the man's world of baseball, but because she had no interest in baseball and already had at the age of 36 a reputation in magazine publishing. He assumed she'd stick with magazines where she had built a successful career—until she spoke up: "What about me? I think this is the right time and place for me."

As with anything you start, you must understand the concept, know the competition, know the market penetration and know what your customers want.

A major decision faced the two-career couple. During their 11 years of marriage, each was already a success on his or her own in separate careers. Together, they had invested on the side in a minor-league team to fulfill Tom's dream. Sherrie once asked him, "If you could do anything in the world, what would it be?" His ready answer was: "Own a baseball team." Now he had his team, but he needed someone else to take on the task of making his dream a profitable enterprise while he remained with the Leo Burnett Advertising Agency in Chicago as a high-paid executive vice president. Sherrie understood his hesitation about surrendering to her the reins of a team he dreamed of owning, but she was also confident of her skills as an entrepreneur.

Here it was his dream and I would now be working at it full-time rather than he. That's a little hard to swallow. After he said, "Maybe you're right," about my running the startup in Lansing, he asked how it would work. Then I described what I would do to get the startup going. I would finish writing the business plan and write up the operations plan. I'd do the initial hiring, organize the retail set-up, do all the sales planning and train the people. I figured that I'd be out by July. We agreed that when we started to make money, I would be paid a consulting fee; I wasn't volunteering my time. So from February 1995 on, I spent 80 percent of my time in Lansing. But by July there was no way I could pull out. Things got bigger than we had ever expected.

What emerged from the start-up is arguably the most successful minor-league team in baseball history. Called the Lansing Lugnuts, the team set the all-time minor-league record for first-year Class A attendance by drawing 538,326 fans in 1996 to newly built Oldsmobile Park (and have stayed above 500,000 since then). Until then, no Class A team had ever reached 500,000 in its first season. Among all 156 U.S. minor-league teams, only 3 teams had higher attendance in 1996. Revenues from 1997 sales of team merchandise ranked No. 1 in all of minor-league baseball, even outselling several major-league teams.

When Tom took a six-month leave of absence in February 1996 to help get the Lansing operation rolling, he and Sherrie began working side by side for the first time since their college days at the University of Missouri. Twenty years before, as fellow students in an advertising course, they created calendars and sold space to local businesses, netting $5,000. This time around, he was supposed to return to a high-powered job in which he reported directly to the chairman of the agency and handled Fortune 100 clients like Procter & Gamble, Kellogg's, Nintendo, and Hallmark. Soon, Sherrie and Tom were agonizing over a decision for him to quit. His six-figure salary was their safety net. If he quit, they would become all-or-nothing entrepreneurs.

He quit.

Sherrie and Tom mean business, Tom's love of the game notwithstanding. (His own baseball career reached its peak at age 12 when he pitched a no-hitter for his Little League team.) A detailed business plan established the four cornerstones for their Lansing operation:

1. We are primarily in the business of entertainment, not the sport of baseball. Tickets will be reasonably priced, with the experience of coming to the game superseding what happens on the field.
2. We will hire and train the best employees.
3. We will build the entire operation around customer service.
4. We will strive to become a permanent and constructive citizen of mid-Michigan.

The Lansing Lugnuts mission statement sums it all up: "To provide affordable, innovative entertainment and positively outrageous service while building a lasting relationship with our community."

The entrepreneurial formula was clear from the start. It's not what happens on the field that counts so much as how the people in the stands feel. It's not the score that counts; it's the experience. It's not a sport; it's a business that makes people feel good. Fellow entrepreneur Mary Ellen Sheets, whose successful moving franchise, Two Men and A Truck, is also based in Lansing, sums up her experience as a Lugnuts ticket holder: "The fans have such a good time at the ball park that they leave feeling great without being sure who won or lost." Sherrie agrees:

"Half of the people leave the game not knowing what the score was, but they had a good time."

Minor-league baseball can offer something bigger than who wins or loses. Sherrie sees the Lugnuts as bringing "something special for people in Lansing who've always loved baseball but haven't had it in their back-yards. . . . It's for parents and grandparents to take their children and grandchildren to the ball park. We're creating memories for people." What has made the busi-ness a success is a formula that Disneyland epitomizes: Offer children of all ages a good time and memorable, family-based experiences, and they will come back time and time again.

For Sherrie and Tom, the road to Lansing was no joyride. They paid their dues. They spent a year network-ing in the self-centered world of minor-league baseball, learning its inbred ways, making contacts, and looking for a franchise to buy. When it comes to owning a minor-league franchise, Sherrie's business-before-baseball for-mulation was on target.

> It's very confusing the way it works in the minor leagues. The only thing we have to do with the major league club [formerly the Kansas City Royals, now the Chicago Cubs] is a Player Development Contract, which gives us the right to have their players play for us. It's very confusing, and the average person doesn't understand it. The owners of a minor league franchise own the operation, the business if you will. The contract is with a major league team that has the right to recruit, pick and train players and send them to us to play. The major league team pays the players and decides who comes down to us and who goes up to the majors. We have nothing to do with that. We sell the seats, open the gates, service the fans. We also pay for the uniforms and bats and balls and for travel,

but we don't have anything to do with the actual base-ball side of the operation.

As a team owner, you market entertainment. We're a single A team which is not what you call a very refined level of play. The pitcher could be fantastic one night and the next time unable to find the plate. That's one reason you can't market around players, not to mention that the major league team could decide a player is gone and he's history in 24 hours.

Fear is something you have to deal with personally. . . . If you're not scared, then you don't realize the risks you're taking. . . . Conviction, believing in what you're doing, is what gives you the energy to go ahead and deal with the risks.

As investors, the first step for Sherrie and Tom was to buy a franchise amidst the intense competition for minor-league teams. Thanks to their networking, Tom learned that the Waterloo Diamonds were for sale—a team that drew only 500 fans on a good day, was losing $100,000 a year, and was playing in a run-down stadium. Its 13 owner-partners were not interested in spending the money needed to upgrade the stadium to meet new standards that had been established. They wanted to sell. Despite the team's anemic condition, the lure of owning a baseball team had attracted nine groups of potential investors when Dickson rushed in with an offer to buy. As far as he's concerned, one reason he won out is that he flew to Waterloo and met personally with the owners rather than use a broker as a stand-in. (Sherrie encourages all entrepreneurs to use such a face-to-face approach.) He also offered the cleanest contract—free of conditions, stipulations, and escape clauses.

Sherrie and Tom still hadn't raised the $2 million needed to buy the franchise and establish credit lines to cover operating costs. They used their own money to make the down payment (which they risked forfeiting) and were ready to put all the money they had into the purchase. Sherrie identifies the risk taking as "part of being an entrepreneur." The couple talked to everyone in their baseball network in search of prospects to put on their money list of investors. The limited liability corporation they set up had five ownership units, each of which could have several participants. Tom took the lead in doggedly presenting the case for investing based on a plan to relocate the team to a profitable setting. He was helped by the readiness of investors in sports teams to accept bottom-line uncertainties. "These are guys," Sherrie says, "who always said they'd give anything to own a baseball team."

Nothing was easy. First a nail biter—the financing wasn't nailed down completely until the day the deal closed. Then a shocker—six weeks before opening day in 1994, Waterloo's city fathers reacted against the idea that the team had been unloaded and would be eventually relocated. They suddenly announced that the token $1 annual lease for their rickety stadium was being raised to $500,000. Sherrie remembers it as a time of panic.

> *I remember vividly our conversation. Tom said that the situation was ridiculous. "The numbers just won't work." I remember saying that we had to move the team and he said that we didn't have time. I said that the only way to problem solve is piece by piece. Let's take it one step at a time. Don't worry about things like the name of the team in a new location or about selling tickets. We need a roof over our head and we can't pay half a million in rent for it.*

Where is there a roof? You're limited by regulations and restrictions that you wouldn't believe. We looked at the geography limiting the location of the 14 teams in the Midwest League and, with help from the league president, George Spelius, located a roof in Springfield which had a team that moved elsewhere. George was just great. He suggested an emergency re-location and helped us get approval, which normally takes six months. Tom flew to Springfield, met with the mayor and they signed a two-year lease with a third-year option.

Then we needed a name so we could sell tickets. Tom and I happen to be into alliteration so we went through the dictionary under S and came up with the Sultans of Springfield. We got an illustrator to come up with a logo in 24 hours. Were things perfect? No. But we had to move fast. I flew down to Springfield and tried to sell advertising signage at the ball park. I told people they had 48 hours to get back to us, first come, first served. People laughed at us, but we did sell a fair amount of advertising, considering the market. Meanwhile, we hoped that Springfield would wake up and decide to build a new stadium, because the facility is everything to success in baseball. The experience at the ball park must be entertaining, but it begins with the facility. We had hopes that Springfield would come through with a new facility, but within six months we knew that it was almost impossible. There were a few fans in the community, but not enough to support a long-term franchise. When we knew Springfield wasn't going to cut it, Tom began calling people and networking in search of a place to relocate the team and get a new stadium. This led us to Lansing's mayor, David Hollister, who said, "I've got it. I understand. Let's see if we can make this happen."

In Lansing, Sherrie and Tom found a city ready to make a long-term commitment to a professional team. Lansing was already exploring the idea of getting its own minor-league team. It's the state capital, large enough to support a team and it was hungry for one. Whereas Sherrie found Lansing an appealing place to live, she was surprised to hear people in the community complain that "there's nothing to do in Lansing." It was an attitude that spelled opportunity for a team. In addition, Lansing is relatively close to Chicago, where Tom was still working with the Leo Burnett Agency. The city itself, which has a strong community spirit, was in the midst of revitalizing the downtown area and had a supportive mayor out to strengthen his preelection popularity by leading the way in getting state and federal financing to help build a new stadium.

I just sat down and tried to figure out what team merchandise to buy. I talked to friends who had been in retail and had been buyers and tried to come up with a formula to decide on how much of my budget to allocate to such items as T-shirts, sweatshirts and baseball hats. . . .

With Waterloo out of the picture, a double play was executed. While the team played out the 1995 season in Springfield on a shoestring with a skeleton crew, Sherrie geared up for opening day 1996 in Lansing. It was two years of red ink in Springfield for the limited-liability corporation before the team was relocated.

For starters, the team needed a new name, so Sherrie ran a "Name the Team" contest in Lansing and created a citywide buzz about the choice with radio and newspaper ads and stories. Not surprisingly, 70 percent of the suggestions were linked to Lansing's automotive history. The name Lugnuts came up repeatedly. "In the end, Tom and I made the decision," Sherrie says. "We knew we had to use a name that was campy, quirky and fun, that could interact with a fun mascot, that could be appealing on merchandise, that could have long-term appeal and even national visibility. The people in the community got around to realizing that the name was actually celebrating Lansing—rather than making fun of it, as critics of the name complained at first."

The name itself created another problem when the requisite trademark search showed that Hasbro Toys already had the rights to the name. Sherrie phoned directly to the giant toy company's chairman and was put in touch with an assistant to whom she pleaded her case. After going through company channels, she received permission and could develop a line of merchandise featuring the Lugnuts logo, establish a mascot—The Big Lug (looking like a two-legged dinosaur stuffed into a baseball uniform). The team's colors became scarlet, black, and silver, and its motto became "Lansing Lugnuts—Where Everyone Gets to Play." Next, Sherrie had to go shopping for logo-bearing merchandise.

> *Baseball teams tend to think of team merchandise as novelty sales at a souvenir stand. Maybe that's because it's dominated by men. They don't think in terms of how many items you can sell someone, of whether to have zippers down the front, contrasting collars, etc. We don't regard it as a souvenir business. We regard it as a retail business. That sounds normal, but you'd have to look at other baseball operations to see how unusual that is. We have polo, denim and*

khaki shirts, golf sweaters and shorts, and jackets, as well as glow sticks, glassware, pencils, pen knives and, of course, baseballs. It's a real store. I've defined it as merging the best of baseball with the best of The Gap. If you go to The Gap and then come back two weeks later, the items on the shelves have completely turned over, which makes customers feel as though they must come back or they'll miss something. That's how we run our stores.

I just sat down and tried to figure out what team merchandise to buy. I talked to friends who had been in retail and had been buyers and tried to come up with a formula to decide on how much of my budget to allocate to such items as T-shirts, sweatshirts and baseball hats. I didn't know if 20 percent of my budget for sweatshirts was too much or too little. Should 30 percent go into hats? What about adjustable hats? The association for minor league teams didn't have a set of guidelines as a model to follow. So I basically guessed what to stock up on and eventually developed my own model of what to buy based on what sold. I hired Mary Kay Schultz who had spent 13 years in buying and management at Spiegel, Inc. and we made the second buy together. Then gradually, she took over all the buying. That's very common with entrepreneurs. You bring somebody along and you try to pull back as much as you can, using checks and balances. You guide, communicate and then turn things over. Mary Kay does it all now and I don't even see the orders before she places them. She is fantastic and was eager for the opportunity.

Sherrie went all out to build a brand name more than a year before opening day in Lansing on the principle that "whatever you're selling, branding drives buying behavior." She had to create demand for something that didn't yet exist: a team without a name that was going to play in a stadium that hadn't been built yet. If an entrepreneur can be defined as creating a profitable business where none existed before, it happened in Lansing.

> *What we did applies to any entrepreneurial effort well before you deliver product or service. We weren't going to deliver the experience of the game until April of 1996, but we went after up-front exposure starting in the spring of 1995. We wanted to build awareness to stimulate people to make buying decisions whether it be merchandise, advertising or tickets. We created a brand and around that brand we created expectations that it was going to be much more than baseball. There was the hoop-la about naming the team and the attention created by the opening of our retail store. All around town, people were talking about the name for the team, speculating and wondering what it would be. We created a community-wide sense of expectation.*
>
> *In May 1995 when we opened Nuts & Bolts, our retail store, we had a stage set up in downtown Lansing and the streets were closed down. We announced the name of the team, the mascot jumped out of a box, the mayor spoke, a ribbon was cut and customers poured into the store. It was a phenomenal success. We had lines three blocks long of people coming to buy team merchandise. We sold an ungodly amount of merchandise in the Thursday, Friday and Saturday of the store's opening weekend, something like $200,000. The FedEx delivery people couldn't get through the crowds. They had to make their deliveries to an empty space at an adjacent retailer. We created brand around the look and the feel of the logo, which was on all the team merchandise we sold. People were walking around, wearing team hats, shirts, sweaters as walking advertisements for the Lugnuts.*
>
> *Our target audience is adults aged 25 to 54, with families. I'd say that 60 to 70 percent of our retail buy-*

ers are mothers who buy for themselves, their children or their spouses. We had $1 million in retail sales in 1996 and 1997. We've sold over 70,000 hats alone and they're obviously not worn only by kids. We've even sold them all over the world through our Web site. Everyone wearing one of our team products became signage.

Until the brand was established, I wouldn't sell tickets or advertising. I'll never forget a phone call from a company that is now one of our biggest advertisers. In late spring of 1995, its advertising manager desperately wanted to buy a "sign" at the ball park advertising his company. I told him we weren't ready. He couldn't believe it. He was afraid of being shut out. I told him that I would put him on the list, but I wouldn't talk about advertising before August and would be happy to talk to him then. He couldn't believe we wouldn't take his money. He called around town in disbelief. As it turned out, when the time came he spent twice as much for advertising at the park as he originally intended, thanks to the build-up for the brand and the fact that we didn't just sell him a "sign."

To sell tickets we used direct marketing based on our retail sales and generated a database. We had someone at the store door handing out customer forms so we had the names and addresses of everyone from the first customer on. From then on, we built up our database for direct marketing of tickets. We don't use newspaper advertising. We're much more targeted than that. We use a database of everyone who ever bought team merchandise and market to them by mail.

Sherrie's database includes the names and addresses of customers; home and work telephone numbers; and also the names, addresses, and ages of family members. Lugnuts doesn't sell tickets to fans; it opens "accounts." Sherrie didn't rush to sell tickets, either. They couldn't be bought until the August after the opening of the Nuts & Bolts store. It was called Red Hot Tickets, and the offering came in different varieties: from individual tickets, season tickets, and luxury suites to packages of 10 and 20. Tom and Sherrie lived up to their commitment to reasonable ticket prices: from $3.50 to $7.

When the game starts it's like a curtain going up on a play. If you were the person running the theater you would have to be at the play. To me that's the only way in event marketing to run a good business—which is really what this baseball team is. So during every game I'm not sitting. I'm working the game. . . .

Along with the brand, the partnership of Tom and Sherrie, as the team's cofounders, became well defined. "I'm a business person with a focus on sales," Sherrie says. "Tom is the one with a vision as well as the one who handles all operations and finances. I'm the one with pages of *To Do* lists. He concentrates on the big picture. His *To Do* list has five things on it." In running all the sales-related activities—tickets, retail sales of team merchandise, and advertising—Sherrie gives top priority to the customer. In the stands, ushers (called concierges) have complete authority to do whatever it takes to make fans happy, whether it involves replacing a cold hot dog with a hot one or moving them to a different seat if they don't like the one they have.

Every employee always carries a customer comment card to take down customer feedback, name, and phone number for relay to the director of customer service (a rarity in baseball). Within 24 hours, everyone filling out a card or phoning in comments gets a personal call back. Six surveys a year keep a finger on customer pulse and regular focus groups tap fan feelings, complaints, and suggestions. A typical example of what Sherrie calls "little things that make a big difference" is the service provided season ticket holders. They can be reached at a phone number at Oldsmobile Park. If called, a concierge delivers a cellular phone to their seat so they can talk to the caller.

Sherrie is clear about the business amidst all the fun. She identifies it as "event marketing—like putting on 70 weddings a year for 10,000 people a night." What happens at the ballpark is planned and choreographed down to the minute, particularly the empty time between each half inning. Everything is set down in a detailed game plan that would make the most meticulous movie director look haphazard. For the Friday, July 24, 1998, game with starting time of 6:05 P.M., the game plan began at 5:30 P.M. with a VIP welcome, followed by music at 5:32, a "Moonwalk," and announcements; at 5:38, speed pitch, Pepsi video, baseball giveaway registration, and batting cage; at 5:45, starting lineups and umpires. And so it goes, all charted on a master plan with headings for time, inning, PA announcements, music, and scoreboard animation.

The happenings between innings included sling shot (free T-shirts propelled into the crowd), mascot race, Frito Lay races, hot dog cannon (wrapped hot dogs shot into the stands), "Sumo" wrestling, impersonations, and, postgame, Conga line. (Seven times a season, there are postgame fireworks.) Then, there are the added touches, like playing "Three Blind Mice" when the umpires appear; or whipping up the crowd with the theme from *Rocky;* or the appearance of a ground keeper in red mechanic's overalls, who shines the plate umpire's shoes and bald head with a garage rag.

Sherrie and the rest of the staff are continually looking for crowd pleasers to insert into the ball game: Fans in boxing shorts put on giant gloves and engage in slapstick matches; or they volunteer to be human bowling balls and, heavily padded, roll down a ramp; or they compete for a dozen doughnuts as the prize for singing the next line of the song "Go Nuts for Donuts." A favorite on kids' day is the "Sunday Sundae Eating Contest" when children sit on top of the dugout and compete to see who can finish eating a sundae first—without using utensils. The crowd loves it.

In running the organization, Sherrie and Tom combine empowerment of employees with their own day-to-day involvement. They're at the ballpark for almost all the season's 70 games. Tom's responsibilities for operations include close oversight of the food stands, which carry appropriate automotive names—Hub Cap Cafe, Chrome Plated Grille, Dashboard Diner—and serve up fan favorites like the ethyl dog or the diesel dog. Sherrie is out in the stands, wearing her Lugnuts cap and mixing with the fans, backing up her concierges, doing whatever it takes to make customers happy. She and Tom also hand out "Lugnuts Loot"—gift certificates to concierges whom she spots making an extra effort to serve fans.

As far as Sherrie is concerned, "sales is in my blood." Her father owned a series of businesses: upholstery company, aviation parts company, mobile home dealership. She saw firsthand what it takes to throw yourself into a business; work never bothers her: "I love working. When people ask what's my hobby, I have to respond by saying 'work'." In college, at the University of Missouri, she studied marketing and advertising before beginning her career in 1979 at the *Chicago Tribune* where she became a national account representative. Next, she joined a publishers rep firm that handled ad sales for several magazines. From there, she got into the start-up business by helping *Smithsonian* magazine launch *Air and*

Space, then helped launch a health/lifestyle magazine, *Hippocrates* (which is now known as *Health Magazine* and is owned by Time-Warner). Her next venture involved the first-ever magazine for salespeople, *Selling.* The latter experience left a bitter taste when she became caught up in corporate politics and in people policies she didn't agree with. She turned to consulting while deciding on her next move. She was weighing offers to run magazines in New York or to do another start-up when she and Tom talked baseball on that December evening in an Evanston Italian restaurant. In retrospect, what has happened is not so much the conversion into a baseball addict of a woman once bored by Chicago White Sox games that she attended with her husband as the discovery of what baseball can mean to people.

> *With the Lugnuts, we have forever changed the community. It doesn't have the same state of mind that it had before the Lugnuts came to town. The team has made a difference. People have a great time at the ball park. I see in kids' faces that they are absolutely thrilled—because we create memories that they would never have had. I walk around the stands wearing a fanny pack with autographed balls in it. I'll hand out a ball if I see a child who has spilled a drink or a child who is crying or if I see a cute child or a group from XYZ Church or school or whatever.*
>
> *When the game starts it's like a curtain going up on a play. If you were the person running the theater you would have to be at the play. To me that's the only way in event marketing to run a good business— which is really what this baseball team is. So during every game I'm not sitting. I'm working the game. I'm seeing and talking to people enjoying themselves. The game goes very fast now. There's not a boring moment in our games. You can ask anyone in Lansing.*

Sherrie regards what she's doing as a template for any start-up, applicable to any entrepreneurial effort. She identifies four phases:

1. Homework
2. Advice
3. Fear
4. Conviction

> *I wasn't insecure not knowing about baseball. Basically, I applied what I did in all my other start-ups, the four stages starting with homework. We created a business plan, a 140-page document that we update every year. Having started other businesses, I knew how important the business plan is. We also set up an operating plan for the stadium that was being built, right down to who's going to be doing what, when and where. In preparing the business plan, I tried to find out what the average new team does in this size market. Attendance of 350,000 sounded like the logical number at that time, but, as it was, we blew that number out of the water. As with anything you start, you must understand the concept, know the competition, know the market penetration and know what your customers want. For instance, when advertisers asked for rate cards, we told them: "We don't have rate cards. Tell us your needs. We need to know your marketing objectives and only then can we work together to meet them."*
>
> *After the homework comes the advice. You pick the brains of people you really value, a narrower universe than the people you talked to in doing your homework. These would be people who could identify areas of problems. In our case, a baseball broker with his broad experience was very helpful as was someone who runs a large retail operation. We wanted to know about the cash flow we could expect from our*

retail operation. You talk to your bankers, but cautiously. They only want to lend you money if they think you don't need it. You get an idea about whether you can get more money down the road to expand. Some people warned me that minor league baseball is the worst of the old boys' network. Wrong. It's all in the way you approach them. If you are genuine, you'll win them over.

Fear is something you have to deal with personally. For instance, at one point in August 1995, we were dollars from not making payroll. You think of one What If *after another. Probably my father helped me most in teaching me to get over fear by making me realize that you* should *be scared. If you're not scared, then you don't realize the risks you're taking. Think about backing up your fears two or three ways and that you will ease your fears. Such as having another line of credit with another bank.*

Conviction, believing in what you're doing, is what gives you the energy to go ahead and deal with the risks. What counts is preparing yourself. Bobby Knight, the Indiana basketball coach, has a great line: "Everyone has the will to win, but few have the will to prepare to win." For me, with every business I've started, when I was prepared, had done my homework and experienced the fear, I have conviction because I've covered all the problems. I would know if it's a really bad idea. Not that to say that I couldn't fail, but I have the feeling that failure is not an option.

Personally, Sherrie has come to realize two things:

1. "I know I can't work for someone else."
2. "Owning a business with my husband means that we can both be on the same page and it gives us the flexibility to control our own destiny, to literally pick and choose what we want to do."

In Tom, the baseball devotee, and Sherrie, the baseball bystander, the Lugnuts story has a moral for all entrepreneurs: You don't need to know a business, you need to know how to do business. "Tom and I have been able to take our business experience and move into an industry which traditionally hasn't operated in a business-like way," Sherrie says. "We intend to take that cumulative knowledge of applying business practices to the field of sports and run with it." Probably another baseball team or possibly a hockey team. Whatever the next venture, it will be a joint effort, now that Tom has discovered Sherrie as a working partner who has start-up know-how that she can apply anytime, anywhere.

12

DEBORAH JOHNSTON— CARE ADVANTAGE, INC.

"The Kind of Care Giver I Would Want for My Own Mother"

Deborah Johnston—
Care Advantage, Inc.

"The Kind of Care Giver
I Would Want for My Own Mother"

A nurse's determination, a father's advice, and a lawyer's know-how intersected when the newly opened Care Advantage, Inc., of Virginia came to the rescue of two elderly sisters who were living together in their own home and wanted to keep it that way. As recalled by Deborah Johnston, this was one of the earliest examples of how her home health care company delivered on her company motto, "Our Advantage *Is* Caring." The message in the motto is a cornerstone of her success as an entrepreneur in the business of caring for others. Both sympathetic and practical, she's filling a special niche in the highly competitive, incredibly complicated, and emotionally charged field of health care. It's not easy.

When I started Care Advantage in 1988, I was doing nursing visits myself and one of our first cases was two sisters in their eighties. Everybody in their family wanted to put them in a nursing home. But these ladies wanted to stay in their own home and we made that possible. What was interesting to me is that Eula, the older sister, had the will power to tell the family to just buzz off. She really knew what she wanted to do and we were able to help her make that happen. We had people come and fix the roof, we bought their groceries, took them to their doctor's appointments. We took care of everything for them.

It's very interesting about people when they've been together a long time. When one of them dies, it's not uncommon for the other one to go fairly quickly afterwards. That's what happened in this situation. After Eula died, the family just honed in to put the second sister in a nursing home. She died two weeks later, one night before she was supposed to go to a home.

Right from the start, this is what we've been doing—tailor-making services for people. Sometimes they need to be taken to a doctor's appointment or chemotherapy. Sometimes, round-the-clock nursing. Sometimes they just need to have their house cleaned. No one client is quite the same. That's why we have a nurse go out to assess what each individual needs before we undertake care. What the nurses report back can be so different and so unpredictable, depending on the situation: "Only wants a male nurse. . . ." "Needs housecleaning taken care of. . . ." "Has four dogs that need caring for." Or: "Husband very upset because wife died of cancer, need to help support him through this. . . ." "This is really going to be tough. 36-year-old woman is dying of cancer and she's got three small children. Need to send the right type of person."

Ten years after coming to the rescue of Eula and her sister, Care Advantage is a thriving, statewide health care organization with a distinctive approach, 2,000 care givers, a headquarters staff of 50, and eight branches. Patient needs dictate the care provided by different levels of skilled personnel, not rules and regulations, not standard lengths of time for visits. Care Advantage calls it home care without limits, and business has boomed, reaching $10 million in 1998.

[Employees] want flexibility and they want to be appreciated . . . They just like to have some control over their own destiny and where they're working. I just try to treat them well.

It's a special kind of business, certainly not a product and not your usual kind of service, even in the health care industry. It's a combination of personal mission, collaborative effort, and meeting a demand for home-based, patient-centered care. Also, as a business, it's still something of a surprise for Johnston: "I am constantly astonished by the growth of our company. Who could have imagined that it would grow from a couple of sheets of paper to a statewide operation with multiple sites across Virginia in just a few years?"

From the start, Johnston was ready to respond to the full range of patient needs, from fixing the roof to round-the-clock care at home. Typically, nursing agencies schedule visits of four or eight hours and provide standardized services—as distinct from Care Advantage whose visits are only as long or short as needed and defined by each particular situation. In identifying this policy as a cornerstone of her success, Johnston says: "Though nontraditional, our approach has enabled us to focus on the true needs of our patients. We put our patients and our employees first."

Her venture into patient-centered care can be traced to what she saw as an administrative nurse in ambulatory surgery. Johnston watched patients go home "sooner and sooner, sicker and sicker"—still needing health care. She was bedeviled by the thought, "There's got to be a better way." She was determined that any health care business she started would be sensitive to the needs of both patients and nurses, responding to the needs of one and the professional commitment of the other. Growing up as the oldest of six children (five daughters and a son who was the youngest and a twin), she was introduced to care giving from childhood, though she became a nurse because of her father's practical advice.

> *My parents struggled raising six kids. I had a really good dad who gave me a lot of insights. He was the one who talked me into being a nurse. I really wanted to be a secretary. He said that as a nurse you'll always be able to take care of yourself, no matter what happens. It's a great career and you'll always have a job. I did what he told me and it certainly has worked out.*

. . . You must value your employees. Your employees make your business with what they do and what they believe in.

Her brother Michael identifies her determination as a "family trait that's more prominent in Debbie than anyone else in the family." That's how the children were raised. "If you have something to do, you don't do it halfway. If you want to try something, go do it. Get it done. Debbie has huge determination and she wants to be the best that she can be in whatever she does." Michael cites his father's influence. "My father, who was an electrician, was always teaching us things. He would always say that you can't do things without an education and the only way to really be successful is to own your own business."

Johnston's start-up equation included a lawyer with capital as well as know-how. He provided $120,000 in funding to set up an office and fund operations. He also insisted on a five-year business plan, which Johnston hated but now credits as crucial. "Now when I talk to anyone about starting a business, I say that a business plan is the first thing to do. It's like a map, a vision of where you're going." He also helped her navigate the requirements of a no-compete clause with a health care agency that she had administered, then left, feeling unappreciated for her efforts and critical of the arms-length way its owner operated. He was around less and less as Johnston spent more and more time at the office, running the operation. She "barely saw him," and when she tried to develop a bonus system for the nurses he wanted no part of it.

Looking back, she identifies her nurse's training and experience as ideal preparation for running a health care agency with an approach that is both practical-minded and tender-hearted. You have to take care of business, and you have to care about the patients.

> *As nurses, we're really basically sensitive people or we wouldn't be in what we're in. But to function you can't be so caught up in emotions that you can't do your job. You've got to deal with everything from birth to death. When I look back on it, nursing school prepares you for business. You've got to convince people to do things they don't want to do, like roll over I'm going to give you a shot.*
>
> *While I was running a health care agency for someone else, I remember talking to my sister, Jill, who had worked part-time for me in that company. I said I want to start my own company. I didn't know if I could do it or not. I was scared that I was going to fail. I was terribly afraid of not succeeding. I remember this over-*

whelming fear that I wouldn't make it. I remember thinking: "What am I going to do if I don't make it, if we lose all our money?" Then I would go to the gym, exercise and tell myself powerful affirmations.

I went to EST just before I started my own business. It helped me get rid of some of my negative chatter. I don't like the structure of EST sessions because it's very confining, but what they teach are good principles. It's about that chatter in everyone's mind which tells you that you can't do something when you know that you can. It helps you overcome what stops you in life.

For six months after quitting the health care agency, Johnston did her research, made her contacts, and prepared to launch her own business. She visited health care agencies, even worked for some of them as a registered nurse. She saw firsthand how they treated staff, where they sent nurses on assignment, and got to know health care agencies "backwards and forward." She recognized a niche in a market: open-ended, customized home health care instead of such typical requirements as a four-hour minimum when only a bath or a ride was needed. Meanwhile, she worked on the hated business plan that led up to the day in April 1988 when she opened her first office in Richmond with three full-time employees, including her sister, Jill Klinchock.

We opened the doors and business just skyrocketed. I made phone calls to all the people I knew in the field, all the contacts I'd made over my 18 years in nursing, especially social workers. They are the ones who make discharge plans when patients leave the hospital. I asked them to please help me: "I'm scared, I'm afraid I'm not going to make it and I really just would appreciate your supporting me and giving me a chance." And they really did.

On top of that, nurses who were with me at the other company joined my company. As a nurse, I think like a nurse and I know what nurses want. So I tried to create an environment that would be appealing to them. As our business exploded, we had payrolls just going through the roof, which made me really nervous because we were running out of cash from the initial investment. I had my sister go out to the different places where we had accounts, bring along donuts, and talk to them about our newness and about how quickly we needed to be paid. Her visits helped in getting them to pay us faster.

When I started Care Advantage, I was doing nursing visits myself and one of our first cases was two sisters in their eighties. . . . We had people come and fix the roof, we bought their groceries, took them to their doctor's appointments. We took care of everything for them. . . . Right from the start, this is what we've been doing—tailor-making services for people. . . .

As the business defined itself, Care Advantage zeroed in on patients at two ends of the health care spectrum: those who can afford to pay on their own for services and those who depend on state-funded Medicaid Personal Care that carries the option of staying home rather than going to a nursing home. The Medicaid patients, a major part of Johnston's business, can receive up to 10 hours of care a day at home and her company ends up taking care of them for the rest of their lives. Not high-paying but long-lasting, these patients have become a company staple. A significant part of the company's expansion is in the rural areas of Virginia where care is hard to come by and the patients widely dispersed. Some of its nurses cover 40 miles a day to reach patients.

The company has three levels of nurses—certified nursing assistant, licensed practical nurse (LPN), and registered nurse (RN)—and care givers who range from daily helpers to live-in companions. It also provides medical staffers for doctor's offices and medical laboratories. What has emerged is a full spectrum of services, beginning with the company's basic business—patients at home—and extending to physician's offices and hospitals. Johnston speaks from experience in identifying what all her staffers want in their work. "They want flexibility and they want to be appreciated. They don't want to be caught up in the bureaucracy of today's hospital settings. They just like to have some control over their own destiny and where they're working. I just try to treat them well." At Care Advantage, that includes bonuses, a profit-sharing plan, and scholarships so that individuals can upgrade themselves professionally.

In return, Johnston is a stickler for quality control. She has a no-frills definition of what she wants: "The kind of care giver I would want for my own mother."

> *Our employees are, without a doubt, some of the most qualified health care professionals in the state. They take on great responsibility when entering patients' homes and oftentimes are the primary care giver for the patient. They treat patients with the same kindness and respect they would show their own families.*

A series of feedback mechanisms maintain quality. Care Advantage phones new patients to find out how things are going and specially assigned nurses visit them to check firsthand. Patients also get a flyer asking if they're satisfied with their care. After each visit, the patient verifies the number of hours on the care giver's time slip and fills out an evaluation. "We do something that none of my competitors do," Johnston notes. "We put an employee evaluation on each time slip. So that our employees know when they go into a home that the patient is going to evaluate them right there and then."

The care givers are rated on a scale of 1 (low) to 5 (high) for a set of no-nonsense items: planned care completed within shift; uses time well, organizes work; punctuality; attitude; follows requests of patients or supervisor; develops and documents care plan; implements appropriate nursing action; records pertinent data on chart; effective distribution of medication (for LPNs and RNs); follows organization policies and procedure. There's also a space for comments. Johnston points with pride to the comments that turn up: "Does a superior job always. . . ." "Very helpful while husband is in hospital. . . ." "The Best!!!"

> While I was running a health care agency for someone else, I remember talking to my sister. . . . I said I want to start my own company. I didn't know if I could do it or not. I was scared that I was going to fail. . . .

In addition, client surveys probe every part of Care Advantage's services, starting with the quality of service, neatness, punctuality, skills, and attitude. The survey asks if the office staff was courteous and prompt in returning calls, if the nursing supervisor is available and responsive and visits regularly, if the billing department does its job to patient satisfaction. The survey responses, which Johnston watches zealously, also provide the kind of open-ended comments that have built and enhanced Care Advantage's reputation. It is quintessentially the power of the satisfied customer who delivers word-of-mouth recommendations that build the business: "Beverly is a very experienced and hard worker. And she has become a friend of the family. . . ." "Matt was an exceptional young man. I feel very fortunate that we had him. . . ." "The weekend help was excellent. Mary was kind and helpful. Shirley and Tiffany were the type we expected. . . ." "I can't say enough about Tina and Andrea. They worked on a weekend until help was found for my Dad. At a time when my life was upside down, they literally saved me. They both are a definite plus to your company."

The feedback mechanisms build, maintain, and strengthen the company culture of care giving in the way that Johnston always intended—taking care of *the* person, not just looking after a patient.

> *I'm very honest with people and I've taught my staff to be this way: if home care is not the answer for them, I'm not going to try to sell it to them. We don't need to take advantage of people to get business. But we do need to take care of them, whatever they need. I remember when we were starting out there was a man in his eighties who was living alone. It was so sad. He had nobody. I mean nobody. He fell in his bathtub and had been lying there four days before he was found by a neighbor who checked on him. The neighbor called Social Services and they called us. I went over myself.*

The man didn't have the resources for home health care so we helped find him an appropriate adult home. We went in and had yard sales to help him because he couldn't take along all of his things. So we became that man's family. Helped him get situated. Bought him what he needed for the adult home. Sold off the things that he didn't need. That was a really enriching experience for us.

. . . My struggle as we grow [has been] to keep a mom-and-pop flavor where everyone cares about everyone else. People do better when they really know each other. . . . The bigger the company gets the harder it is to keep a family feeling, but we continuously work at it with a summer hoedown at my house, a Christmas party, awards. . . .

When Care Advantage celebrated its 10th anniversary, Johnston included samples of letters that tell the story of success in her business, which is measured two persons at a time—the patient and the care giver. "Thank you for sending Diondra Jones to help me. She is a darling and I love her very much. . . ." "Can't thank you enough for the wonderful nurses you've sent me. I'm home now and feeling better, but it will still be a long pull. My nurses have become some of my best friends. . . ." "This is a hard letter to write. You made it possible for my wife to live as long as she did. Your kindness and cooperation were wonderful. . . ." "Your nurses were all kind and caring for my husband and me and my family. . . ." "Virginia Johnson has been providing full-time nursing care since I underwent major back surgery four months ago. . . . She has been incredibly dedicated and knowledgeable in terms of my overall health and maintenance during this period. Her reliability and tireless dedication have been incredible and I shall be forever grateful. . . ." "Thank you so very, very much for your care and support at the recent death of my husband. I don't know how I could have gotten through that morning without the support and understanding of caring, loving people. Chris Lopez was so very concerned and dedicated. He and your company have been and will be highly recommended by me."

The files at Care Advantage are filled with such letters, each a testimonial to its care givers, a catalogue of the feelings they must deal with and the significance of the company's designated advantage—*caring*. A woman wrote to Deborah about her hospitalized husband who "wanted to go home to die." On the Monday afternoon that he arrived home, Deborah's nurses were there to take over. "I truly feel," she wrote, "that because of the way my husband and I were handled, the honesty and truthfulness, the gentle care and concern we were given together—not just him—has made his death more easy to bear. Care Advantage made his fight for life more comfortable physically as well as emotionally."

The caring company culture created by Deborah Johnston is family based—her own family and the families of her employees. Besides her sister, Jill, who goes back to the company's opening day, another sister, Wendy, has worked part-time as have Deborah's mother and grandmother as well as former mother-in-law. Her aunt ran one of the branches. Her father has chipped in with his skills as an electrician. Brother Michael came on board in 1993 as vice president of operations after completing his MBA. He was brought in not only for his business training. "Besides his management skills," Deborah says, "he'd grown up with five sisters. Since my company is predominantly women, I knew he would have experience in that regard. So he came and helped me manage the company for three years. After I sent him to a weekly entrepreneur-oriented seminar along the lines of EST, he came back wanting to start his business, which he has. It's an auto transmission business."

I would advise all aspiring entrepreneurs to find something they have total passion for. The kind of thing that wakes you up in the morning and keeps your mind churning at night with excitement. I . . . also recommend having confidence in themselves.

Michelle Richardson, the sister-in-law of Andrea Wharam, who is vice president of planning and development training, started working part-time while a sophomore studying accounting at Virginia Commonwealth University. She has since become vice president of finance, the kind of employee that Deborah wants on staff: "I have always had a preference for students because they are excited and enthusiastic and usually positive. They want to go somewhere. You can teach the business to people and all that stuff, but you can't give them enthusiasm and you can't give them energy. Michelle has those things." There are other sisters-in-law of sisters-in-law and friends of friends on staff. It's the way Deborah likes to build her staff.

A lot of our employees bring in relatives to work for us. I see that as a positive because I'm certainly not going to bring my family into a company that's not a good place to work. This has been my struggle as we grow. I'm trying to keep a mom-and-pop flavor where everyone cares about everyone else. People do better when they really know each other, especially when you're working with women. The bigger the company gets the harder it is to keep a family feeling, but we continuously work at it with a summer hoedown at my house, a Christmas party, awards. Such as the latest one I thought of: Rookie of the Year for the employee who has grown the fastest. What I really like is watching people reach their fullest capacity and I make it a policy of promoting from within.

When I give talks, I stress that you must value your employees. Your employees make your business with what they do and what they believe in. So you have to set the right tone for your people. When I come to work in the morning—sometimes at 7, sometimes at 8—after my early morning workout, I make a point of saying hello to everyone. I'm definitely a walker. I check on things in person. I spend a lot of time in strategy meetings with my staff. Outside the office, I meet with people in the community as sort of an ambassador-at-large. I meet with people one-on-one. I attend lunches. I stay in touch.

Brother Michael, brought on for his management skills, ended up getting a business education from his sister as a "perfect role model." He discovered that in the first three years of running her company Deborah had become an accomplished businessperson: "It's still hard for me to realize how successful and how professional she is and what a quality entrepreneur she is. She affiliates with people who are successful in business and from whom she gets ideas and she generates her own ideas. She's always thinking, always looking for ways to improve her business, to expand her business, to help her employees, to improve their lives. It's not: How much money can I make? It's: How can we run a quality business? How can we be better than the competition? How can we make our customers as satisfied as they can be?

"She knows how to enjoy herself, but she also stays focused, knows how to plan, organize herself, put the right people in the right positions and develop an organizational structure that takes care of itself and is prepared for anything. She never underestimates things like costs, watches expenses and analyzes financial data. She's in command of every part of the business, from the smallest detail to the complicated overall picture, keeping an eye on everything through individuals on staff. She gets involved with her employees, sees how they work, goes to visit them, and she knows just every aspect of the business and stays on top of it.

Whatever I do, if I believe in it, I can succeed. . . . If I don't believe in something I can't go out there and do it. But if I believe in it, there's nothing I can't accomplish.

"She certainly is dynamic and aggressive and energetic and colorful. She's also extremely helpful. She's a complex person in a simple kind of personality that's easy to get along with. She has so many different hats and faces. She can sit there and dissect data and she can show you how to work with someone who's having problems. The things that she does, the people she helps—I don't know how she keeps up with it to be honest with you. In a crowd or anywhere she goes, she stands out. There's a glow about her. You can feel it. I have friends that hadn't met her, didn't know anything about her. After meeting her for the first time and talking to her, I can see their reaction: 'Man, who is that?' "

Deborah's duality—people-oriented and business-minded—showed up in a response to her own mother's feelings of emptiness.

> *Let me talk about my mother. She raised 6 kids, she worked her whole life as a secretary, retired, and then went into this empty nest syndrome. She's like me, tons of energy. Suddenly she was at loose ends. When you've raised kids all your life and they leave home, it's a sad time. So I said, "Mom, would you like to help me a couple of days a week with a patient that's in your neighborhood?" So she started.*
>
> *I really learned something from this. It made her so happy. And I cannot tell you how it completely changed my mother to have something to do. So we're going to recruit empty nesters as a part of our program that we're going to call a "Nanny for Granny." Just because I think they're really valuable employees.*

Besides presenting a model of energy, Deborah's mother walked on the sunny side of the street with a positive attitude that rubbed off on her children. In Deborah's case, there was a struggle to stay upbeat after a painful divorce and the challenge of putting her life together. Overnight, she went from the wife of a successful plastic surgeon with hopes of having children and raising a family to a woman on her own. She knew that whatever life she created would be in nursing. She was a graduate of Johnston-Willis School of Nursing, where she got in the habit of doodling hearts when she got bored in class. (Appropriately, a heart is now her company logo.) She worked nine years as a registered nurse at Richmond's Henrico Doctors Hospital where she became involved in nursing management before leaving to administer a home health care agency. Her main thought in rebounding from the divorce was: "I've got to do something with my life." Step One she identifies as spiritual.

> *The church I go to has taught me a lot about being positive. It's a Unity Church and one of the things it offers is a class on prosperity. It's a great class and I took it at the time I was going through my divorce. By prosperity, it means a lot more than money. It's having what your heart desires. The class teaches you about affirming what you want, about being positive and forgetting what didn't work out because that's baggage which is holding you back. You can call it a kind of spiritual awakening, though when you tell some people about it they look at you as if you've got a square head. But that's their problem, not mine.*
>
> *I begin every day with grateful statements: I am grateful for great health, I am grateful for a great family, I am grateful for a wonderful company, I am grateful for the success of a wonderful company. Then I usually have a particular statement, such as one based on the need to hire a good marketing person. I'm grateful for the applicants coming into my office because I believe that you have to affirm something and have a positive thought before good things happen.*
>
> *One of the things I wanted to do when I started my company was to make things better in health care. When I was running the health care agency for its owner, that included making life better for the nurses. I wanted to do things like put them on a bonus plan. But the owner wouldn't let me. Later, when I started*

my company, the nurses came over and, eventually, he went out of business.

I think women make good business people. Look at their role in life. They have a job, make the baby formula, organize the family events, deal with the in-laws, run the family budget, make plans. People trust them more. They're sensitive to the things going on around them. Being an entrepreneur takes all those things—listening to what people need, planning, budgeting, making decisions.

I would advise all aspiring entrepreneurs to find something they have total passion for. The kind of thing that wakes you up in the morning and keeps your mind churning at night with excitement. I would also recommend having confidence in themselves. "Where there is a will there is a way." Financially, it cost me a lot not to have confidence in myself. I would also recommend going through the exercise of writing a five-year business plan. It's a pain, but when you are done you really know your stuff.

From her vantage point, Deborah sees growth both for her company and for the home health care industry in general. She projects a doubling of revenues to $20 million for her company in the next few years and expects to see a growing number of new providers as changing government regulations force people to buy their own care. Demographics are part of what she sees as a booming industry as the number of older Americans increases sharply and as the large majority are able to exercise their preference for staying in their own homes.

Johnston looks ahead to the formation of her own management company to help new providers of home health care. "We're pros at it and we can help companies that are getting into this area," she says. Wherever she ventures, she no longer has any doubts about succeeding—as long as she believes in it.

Whatever I do, if I believe in it, I can succeed. For example, I do a lot of fund-raising in the community for cancer research. If I wanted to do that as a career, I could do it because it's something I believe in. If I don't believe in something I can't go out there and do it. But if I believe in it, there's nothing I can't accomplish.